THE BEGINNER'S GUIDE TO TINY HOUSES

THE BEGINNER'S GUIDE TO TINY HOUSES

WHAT YOU NEED TO KNOW ABOUT 400-SQUARE-FOOT LIVING

ALEXIS STEPHENS AND CHRISTIAN PARSONS

ROCKRIDGE
PRESS

Interior and Cover Designers: Eric Pratt and Amanda Kirk
Art Producer: Sue Bischofberger
Editor: Annie Choi
Production Editors: Matthew Burnett and Rachel Taenzler
Production Manager: Michael Kay

Illustration: pp. 49-51: ©Remie Geoffroi; pp: ii, vi, x, 12, 34, 56, 74, 88, 108, 124: ©Moloko88/ Shutterstock; Photography: p. 2: ©Colin Field/Alamy Stock Photo; p. 3: ©Greg Vaughn/Alamy Stock Photo; p. 6: ©Lowphoto/Shutterstock; p. 26: ©Kristen Curette & Daemaine Hines/Stocksy United; p. 33: © Tony Anderson/Getty Images; p. 36: ©Taylor Kampa/Stocksy United; p.38: ©J.G. Domke /istock/Getty Images; p. 40: ©Ian Bottle/Alamy Stock Photo; p. 41: ©A.P.S. (UK)/Alamy Stock Photo; p. 60: Kayla Johnson/Stocksy United; p. 62: ©Raul Rodriguez/istock Editorial/Getty Images; p. 63: ©Christian Tisdale/Stocksy United; p. 66: ©Toni Massot/Alamy Stock Photo; p. 67: ©Tari Gunstone /Stocksy United; p. 69: ©Jam Travels/Shutterstock; p. 76: ©Brett Donar/Stocksy United; p. 78: FatCamera/Getty Images; p. 80: ©Leah Flores /Stocksy United; p. 92: © Erik Laan/Shutterstock; p. 96: ©Ian Pratt/Stocksy United; p. 97: ©Pia Simon/Living4Media; p. 99: ©ppa/Shutterstock

Author Photo: Courtesy of Tiny House Expedition

ISBN: Paperback 978-1-64876-828-6 | eBook 978-1-64876-250-5

R0

*This book is dedicated to those who helped
make our tiny-house journey possible and those
who let us share their stories with the world.*

CONTENTS

INTRODUCTION viii

CHAPTER ONE

WELCOME TO THE BIG WORLD OF TINY HOUSES 1

CHAPTER TWO

IS A TINY HOUSE RIGHT FOR YOU? 13

CHAPTER THREE

GOING MOBILE: TINY HOUSES ON WHEELS 35

CHAPTER FOUR

STAYING PUT WITH YOUR TINY HOUSE 57

CHAPTER FIVE

UNCONVENTIONAL TINY HOUSES 75

CHAPTER SIX

MAKING IT HAPPEN 89

CHAPTER SEVEN

DOWNSIZING FOR A TINY HOUSE 109

RESOURCES 125

INDEX 140

Introduction

Hello! We are Alexis Stephens and Christian Parsons, Tiny House Expedition cofounders, and we are thrilled to welcome you to the wonderful world of tiny houses. After falling in love, we built our cozy 130-square-foot tiny house on wheels with the help of friends and family in North Carolina. Then, in 2015, we hit the road on an epic trip across North America to explore the tiny home movement—the diverse people, the pioneering culture, and the community experience. What we initially thought would be a one-year trip became a lasting nomadic lifestyle. And hopefully soon, a tiny homestead!

Our journey to tiny houses began with a burning desire to break free from stress and stagnation. We both stumbled across the movement at different times, despite being lifelong lovers of pillow forts, cabins, and tree houses. But it was our first road trip together that planted the seed of our future minimalist traveling lifestyle. We hadn't been dating long when we took off on a 10-day camping excursion to Lake Michigan. Not only did we love seeing the sights together, but we also discovered how well we worked together in small spaces—living out of a Honda Element and in a small tent. Ultimately, this kick-started a yearlong search for opportunities to simplify and do more adventuring.

Addictive Pinterest scrolling led to more extensive research around the downsized lifestyle. What deeply resonated with us is the idea that simple living can result in a higher quality of life centered around personal priorities. Baked into the concept of living in a tiny house is the permission to tune in to what makes you happy by shutting out the noise of conventional societal pressures and overconsumption habits. We also learned about the many ways tiny houses are being used to creatively address housing shortages, the need for sustainable living, and the desire for more meaningful lifestyles. The idea was born to return to our filmmaking passion by traveling to document tiny-house stories, from the comfort of our very own tiny home on wheels.

In 2014, we began building our DIY tiny house in earnest. We ended up using many salvaged and reclaimed materials—from an old farmhouse, the Habitat ReStore of Forsyth County, and felled trees from a tornado. Processing these materials was labor-intensive, but in the end, we saved quite a bit of money and added much charm and character to our tiny house. Perhaps the best part: Everything in our home has a story behind it.

What a ride it's been since then! During our travels, we called 37 states and one Canadian province our home. We also visited over 30 different kinds of tiny home communities, met hundreds of tiny-home dwellers, and welcomed tens of thousands of people into our tiny home during special events. Our home also became the inspiration behind a children's book, *The Big Adventures of Tiny House.*

The priceless experiences, new friendships, and lessons learned along the way have given us much fulfillment. It's been our great pleasure to share insights and resources with the world on our Tiny House Expedition website and YouTube channel. A favorite is our educational documentary series, *Living Tiny Legally*, about the legal challenges around tiny house living and how they're being overcome through the work of inspiring advocates. These efforts to inspire positive change led us to join the leadership team of two outstanding nonprofits, the Tiny Home Industry Association and the American Tiny House Association.

So basically, you get the picture: We're proud tiny-house nerds!

Curious about tiny houses but don't know much about them beyond their adorability? Perfect. This book is ideal for the true beginner. We're going to break down the fundamentals of the movement and lifestyle in an easy-to-understand way. By the end of this book, you will clearly see what it takes to live tiny and understand the first steps you can take to start your journey.

Our sincere hope is to inspire you with the fulfilling possibilities of simple living in a tiny house so you can decide if it's right for you. If not now, it might be ideal for another chapter of your life. Ready to get started? Let's do this!

CHAPTER ONE

WELCOME TO THE BIG WORLD OF TINY HOUSES

Living in a tiny home is a tale as old as time, but it's experiencing a revival today. The modern tiny-house movement is a cultural movement centered around simplifying one's life in a conscious way—a "less is more" lifestyle. By redefining how much space and stuff it takes to be happy, simple living can offer clarity and solace for the fast-moving world around you.

Besides the endlessly creative designs of the houses themselves, what lies at the heart of the movement is self-empowerment. Tiny-house living opens up the doors to reevaluating how you spend your time and money. Many people find satisfaction in this, realizing that the quality of their relationships and experiences creates the most fulfillment.

As part of your journey, let's explore how a tiny house can help you achieve your goals and live your priorities. In this chapter, you'll learn what exactly we mean by a tiny house, the beginnings of the modern tiny-house movement, and some tangible benefits of the lifestyle.

What Is a Tiny House?

The term "tiny house" gets thrown around a lot, often incorrectly. While there is room for interpretation, a tiny house is typically recognized as a dwelling that is 400 square feet or less, whether on wheels or on a foundation.

A tiny house on wheels (THOW) is a movable tiny house. At its core, a THOW is a hybrid structure. It brings together a travel trailer's mobility with the durable materials and construction techniques of a traditional home, making it suitable for year-round living. A well-built THOW is highly insulated, sturdy, and customizable from the initial build to future home renovations—things that are harder to achieve in RVs. In general, tiny homes tends to be taller, heavier, and less agile on the road than an RV, though there are exceptions. Similar in footprint, both THOWs and travel trailers often utilize 16- to 40-foot-long trailers with an 8½-foot-wide interior, though wider models do exist.

Tiny homes on wheels can include traditional RVs, school bus conversions, and vardos. All wheeled homes can be relocated relatively easily or can even be suitable for full-time nomadic living.

A tiny house on wheels can also be set on a permanent foundation if the wheels are removed. Once you cross over into the stationary category, the style and shape possibilities expand greatly—from classic cabins and dome homes to converted fill-in-the-blanks like grain silos and shipping containers. A few of these options can be relocated, but at significant expense and effort. We'll dig into that later.

No matter what kind of tiny house you choose, it doesn't have to be extremely minimalist. Many people create efficient yet impeccably decorated spaces and what some refer to as "luxury" tiny homes. Each can be customized to meet your needs and personal style.

A tiny house's cost varies considerably based on size, level of customization, and materials used. Despite the vast range, the price of a typical tiny house, especially one on wheels, is significantly lower than that of your average full-size home. For example, a typical DIY tiny house can cost less than $45,000. On the other end of the spectrum, some people spend $125,000 or more for professionally built, upscale, and decked-out tiny homes.

Keep in mind that these costs do NOT include land or associated expenses such as permitting fees, which explains why interest in THOWs has grown exponentially over the last 15 years. Detaching housing from land is a revolutionary concept, which is especially attractive to those who are seeking affordable homeownership, plan to retire on a fixed income, or want flexibility to relocate with their home.

The History of Tiny Houses

Americans tend to forget that living simply and in small structures is a way of life that has been around since the beginning of time, from cave dwellings to pioneer cabins.

Tiny houses have evolved over recent decades and come in many styles, appealing to people from all walks of life, each as unique as the owner, from downsizing retirees, starter home–seeking couples, and minimalist Millennials, to everything in between.

A cornerstone of the movement is the emphasis on individuality, from design to lifestyle, all curated around creating personal fulfillment.

So the common thread that binds the diverse designs and individuals in the modern tiny-house movement is the idea that a tiny home can be a multi-tool. It offers a wide range of quality, affordable, and environmentally friendly housing that can be used to meet personal dreams, financial and lifestyle goals, and community needs.

Because the traditional housing market is incredibly limited, a growing number of individuals and organizations are bootstrapping their own solutions by building or buying tiny houses. Advocates and nonprofits see them as a fill-in-the-gap solution to addressing the need for a more robust housing and shelter spectrum.

THE ROOTS OF THE MODERN TINY-HOUSE MOVEMENT

In the 20th century, you could find multiple examples of small structures popping up to meet housing demand and used as an escape from traditional thinking. These included early mobile homes trying to address post-WWII housing needs and the embrace of simple living in the "back-to-the-land movement" of the late '60s and '70s.

Jay Shafer built his first tiny house on wheels in 1999. Not long after that, he launched the Tumbleweed Tiny House Company and cofounded the Small House Society. In 2006, he received national exposure on *The Oprah Winfrey Show,* the top tastemaker of the time. This media attention allowed tiny houses to enter America's consciousness just in time for the Great Recession.

The housing crisis of 2008 directly contributed to the rise of the modern tiny-house movement. Millions of people downsizing out of necessity slowly led to a robust national conversation around the meaning of home and success—set against the backdrop of a destructive culture of overconsumption, crippling stress, and economic inequality.

For many, a new American Dream emerged, one of reduced debt and greater freedom that can be achieved through tiny-home living. This dream continues to resonate deeply.

TINY HOUSES TODAY

Over the past 15 years, the tiny-house movement grew steadily. It is now worldwide, with massive popularity in Australia and burgeoning in several other countries.

More recently, its popularity exploded, thanks to the significant exposure from the Netflix documentary *Tiny* in 2013, followed by the cable debut of the first tiny house shows in 2014. Together they put the term "tiny house" into mainstream cultural awareness. Around that time, numerous YouTube channels debuted with tiny-home tours and how-to videos.

More and more people from around the world found themselves enamored with tiny-house designs. And the widespread sharing of practical building knowledge paved the way for countless do-it-yourselfers to pursue building their own tiny homes.

Overall, the movement is driven by the growing number of folks ditching the traditional script of "keeping up with the Joneses" for a simpler life. It's not defined by the exact square footage of the house, but rather the attitude and lifestyle: fewer things, more experiences, and a better quality of life.

A PROFILE IN TINY-HOUSE LIVING

Meet Richard Ward, owner of a tiny house that he built in his mid-twenties. Since moving in, he's embarked on epic adventure after adventure, like hiking 2,650 miles on the Pacific Crest Trail. But none of this would have happened if he hadn't first endured a near-fatal motorcycle accident.

"I spent a lot of time in a hospital bed with nothing to do and realized life is short," Richard shared. "After that, I realized I didn't want to do the corporate job and the 40 hours a week and waking up every morning saying I don't want to go to work." His life-changing experience inspired him to go out on his own as a freelance designer, and most importantly, reprioritize his life around his passions.

Ultimately, Richard decided to design and build his own tiny house on wheels to give him the financial and schedule flexibility he sought.

"The tiny-house movement, it's not about the houses. It's about the lifestyle," Richard explains. "For me, the tiny house is freedom. I don't have to work when I don't want to work . . . it's about the life that comes with the house."

He designed a truly ingenious tiny house named Terraform One. Richard built it in just four months with SIPs (structurally insulated panels) as well as an impressive number of salvaged and reclaimed materials. In the end, he crafted a comfortable home that facilitates his favorite hobbies—biking and home brewing—with room for three bicycles and two beer taps.

From road trips to long-distance hikes, Richard has made the most of every day since becoming a tiny homeowner. He also launched a tiny-house design and consulting business to help others achieve their own downsizing dreams. Now, he's onto a new kind of adventure: creating an off-grid homestead community in the Arizona desert.

Why a Tiny House?

For many who join the movement, their motivation is to reduce consumption and pursue a simpler way of life. Tiny-home living can help create a higher quality of life by better utilizing your time, energy, and finances.

Tiny houses epitomize the saying "less is more." The less available space, the more creative the design. A reduced carbon footprint means greater satisfaction knowing you're doing your part to help the environment. Less house means less cleaning and maintenance, leading to more freedom and abundant life.

IT'S BETTER FOR THE ENVIRONMENT

Housing materials like lumber, roofing, and insulation are essential in building homes. Thus, the bigger the house, the more materials are needed. As the standard home size has increased, so has the amount of new construction waste. Devastating amounts of perfectly good materials end up in landfills every year from material overages.

Tiny houses require fewer construction resources and also produce less building waste because of the individualized construction. Salvage materials are more common, too, reusing what would otherwise be thrown away. As a result, environmental footprints from tiny homes are smaller and help protect the well-being of the environment.

When you go tiny, you further reduce your ecological impact by cutting down energy usage and waste. A 2019 study, "The Ecological Footprints of Tiny Home Downsizers," found that most tiny-home dwellers reduced their energy consumption by 45 percent after downsizing. Many further reduce their carbon footprint through the use of solar power.

For some, the allure of off-grid tiny-house living offers the ultimate freedom through self-reliant sustainability. This can mean creating your own power with wind and solar energy and harvesting your own rainwater. If you enjoy getting your hands dirty, you might relish self-reliant homestead life!

IT SIMPLIFIES YOUR LIFE

Mainstream norms about "socially acceptable" lifestyle choices seem to work against both our awareness of nontraditional ways of living and our confidence in pursuing them. These norms are programmed into us all from a young age via the media, family expectations, and general societal pressures. As a result, the path to "success" in adulthood follows an all-too-familiar series of steps: school, marriage, mortgage, and credit card debt.

The process of transitioning into a tiny house can powerfully reset your perspective on real success, even if you just live tiny for a season of your life. Limiting your square footage naturally limits your ability to collect junk that clutters your home and outlook on life. This literal change of perspective can be key to challenging societal norms and finding personal freedom. Simplicity can also create a higher quality of life. For instance, it often creates extra free time to spend doing what you like, and with the people you love.

Keep in mind that a tiny house is not just for one particular socioeconomic class of people. It can provide value for anyone—from millionaires to those transitioning out of homelessness—because simple homes create opportunities for a more fulfilling life.

IT'S CHEAPER TO MAINTAIN

The actual cost of a traditional home is much more than the mortgage. It encompasses expensive utility fees, long-term maintenance, and repair or replacement costs for things such as roofs and HVAC systems. Plus, the loss of personal time from frequent cleaning sucks hours and hours of your life. All this adds up to an increase in stress that negatively affects your health.

While a larger house requires higher maintenance and related expenses, a tiny house requires the opposite. Living in a tiny home can drastically reduce the amount of money you spend on utilities, maintenance, and repairs. You'll be using less water and electricity than the average homeowner. This will help you save massive amounts over the years, reducing your cost of living.

All the money you don't spend can be dedicated to saving for the future and reducing month-to-month strain. Extra expendable income can also go toward pursuing your passions, like travel or starting your own small business.

While overall maintenance needs and costs may decrease in a tiny house, each surface and piece of furniture in your tiny home will get used more often, resulting in more wear and tear.

IT LETS YOU MOVE WITH YOUR HOME

Tiny houses on wheels originally came about as a means to get around restrictive building codes. THOWs quickly became attractive to many as a mobile asset that can move with you when the need arises.

As a tiny homeowner experiences life changes, like a new job in another state or wanting to be closer to family, they can relatively easily relocate with their home, reducing the heartache and stress of hunting for a new one.

There are challenges to consider when moving your THOWs, such as zoning rules that determine where you can park your tiny home. (More on that in chapter 3.) But generally speaking, picking up and moving is much less of a hassle than with a traditional home.

IT MEETS CRUCIAL HOUSING NEEDS

More people than ever are living alone or nearing retirement age with a fixed social security income. A rapidly growing number of minimalist-minded people find that a well-designed tiny house comfortably suits their needs at a fraction of the cost of market-rate housing. Thus, it provides a higher quality of life, where savings can be used toward healthcare and retirement.

Countless couples and families have used their tiny homes as a stepping stone to save money for a traditional house. Then, the tiny home becomes an asset to house another family member. It can also bring in rental income or even become a vacation home in another location.

Community organizations are popping up to create quality, affordable tiny homes for those in need of stable housing. For example, the Veterans Community Project creates tiny house communities that provide housing and services for homeless vets. Another nonprofit in Detroit, Cass Community Social Services, developed a tiny house neighborhood for minimum wage workers to rent-to-own their own tiny homes. These are just two of dozens of inspiring examples of tiny houses meeting community needs.

Tiny House Communities

Across North America, tiny house communities of varying legal status are cropping up—from intimate backyard co-ops and eco-villages to resort-style developments and residential pocket neighborhoods. Some attract retirees looking to trade in square footage for free time. Others are experiments in how to solve the affordable housing crunch.

BACKYARD COMMUNITY

The most common tiny house parking situation is in an informal backyard community with a traditional house and one or more tiny homes. These sites are typically under the radar, so it is hard to know how many exist. There could be one in your neighborhood!

In a few cases, these backyard arrangements can be a more formal village setup, like Going Places, a tiny cohousing community in Portland, Oregon. A cohousing community is a semi-communal mini neighborhood of private homes clustered around a shared community space. Residents share ownership, maintenance, and resources, like tools and the laundry room. If you seek an intimate, supportive environment, then this may be for you.

Whether you want to establish a collective community vision or prefer a more independent setup, a backyard is perhaps the most accessible model out there. The drawback is that zoning laws don't often accept these types of communities. People who don't have official regulatory approval often end up living under the radar. (More on the perils of this option in chapter 3.)

RV AND MOBILE HOME COMMUNITY

When it comes to tiny houses on wheels, communities like RV and mobile home parks typically provide legal, hassle-free parking with like-minded neighbors. After all, RV and mobile home parks are the original tiny-home communities.

Many parks are reinventing themselves as hybrid RV/THOW communities. This model is the most available and legally acceptable option for tiny-house parking. It features all the necessary amenities for a comfortable on-grid parking experience, with available power, water, and sewer hookups. Depending on the RV park location, the allowed length of stay varies from 30 days to year-round parking.

Another thing to love about this kind of community model is access to outdoor recreational activities and fun points of interest. Do you want to be located in a rural, suburban, or urban setting? In any locale you prefer, you can find an RV or mobile home park.

Be aware that not all of these parks allow tiny houses, and some may require certification. We have stayed in dozens of RV parks across the country and have only been turned away once.

Choose which community is right for you based on your preferences, like location and level of intimacy. Refer to the Resources section (page 125) for help finding your ideal tiny home community or parking spot.

CHAPTER TWO

IS A TINY HOUSE RIGHT FOR YOU?

Many people dreaming of tiny-house living envision a magazine-ready home in a beautiful location, where all their problems disappear as if they're on a permanent vacation. Unfortunately, despite the lifestyle benefits, tiny houses are not for everyone, or even for all phases of life.

What resonates with you the most about the tiny-house lifestyle? Do you want to (finally) own a home, save for big goals, spend more time pursuing your passions, or embark on a new career working remotely? Reflect on what appeals to you most about downsizing. Identifying your priorities is essential to crafting a satisfying lifestyle that's right for you, with or without a tiny home. This chapter will help you sort this out.

Tiny-House-Living Questionnaire

The following questionnaire will help you determine if tiny-house living could be right for you right now. Answer each of the following questions, then total your points to see where you land on the readiness scale.

KNOW YOUR WHY

Knowing *why* you want to live in a tiny home is incredibly important. It can help you figure out whether you have any unrealistic ideas about this lifestyle and how serious you are about pursuing it. Choose your top three reasons.

A: Affordable homeownership

B: Long-term savings

C: It's cute and Instagram-worthy

D: Simplify and reduce stress

E: Design customization

F: To solve all of my problems

G: More free time

H: Environmental reasons

I: Portability

LIFESTYLE

1. **How often do you enjoy entertaining large groups of people (more than three individuals)? Choose one.**

   A: Never/rarely

   B: Frequently (2 to 3 times a month)

2. **How many pets do you have, and how big are they? Choose all that apply. (Skip if not applicable)**

   A: 1 to 3 small dogs

   B: 1 medium–large dog

   C: 2 medium–large dogs

   D: 3 or more medium–large dogs or 3 or more cats

   E: 1 to 2 cats

   F: 1 to 2 small caged animals (fish, reptile, small mammal)

3. **How much storage space do your hobbies require? Choose all that apply.**

   A: Can fit in 1 to 2 drawers

   B: Needs an entire closet

   C: Needs a separate room

   D: Needs a garage

4. **What outdoor recreation activities do you frequently enjoy? Choose all that apply.**

   A: Hiking

   B: Fishing

   C: Cycling

   D: Skiing, snowboarding, or surfing

   E: Rock climbing

LOCATION

1. How do you feel about having neighbors? Choose one.

A: I like living near others.

B: I like living near others and want to know my neighbors.

C: I want to know my neighbors and share resources.

D: I want to live away from others.

2. How open are you to location flexibility? Choose one.

A: I'm entirely open to new places.

B: I prefer to live in a suburban area.

C: I prefer to live in an urban area.

D: I need to live in a specific city.

E: I prefer to live in a rural area.

3. If you're considering a tiny home on wheels, how often do you want to move? Choose one.

A: Just once to my long-term parking spot

B: Rarely, only as needed for big life changes like a new job

C: Snowbird-style, 2 times per year

D: Every 3 to 6 months for work or pleasure

E: Full-time nomads, moving as often as we like

DOWNSIZING

1. Are you willing to part with two-thirds of your belongings (maybe less if you currently live in under 900 square feet)?

Yes

No

2. **If you moved into a tiny house, would you get a storage unit?**

Yes

No

3. **How would you use a storage unit? Choose one. (Skip if not applicable)**

A: For stuff you use regularly but won't have room for, like adventure gear

B: Family heirlooms you feel obligated to hold on to

C: Business supplies and/or inventory

4. **Do you anticipate keeping everything you own?**

Yes

No

5. **Are you willing to sacrifice comforts such as a bathtub or full-size dining table?**

Yes

No

LIVING NEEDS

1. **Who will live in your tiny house? Choose one.**

A: Just me

B: Me and my significant other

C: Me, my significant other, and one pet

D: Me and one child

E: Me, my significant other, and one child

F: Me with three or more other people

2. **Do you work from home?**

   Yes

   No

3. **If you work from home, how much office space do you need? Choose one. (Skip if not applicable.)**

   A: Just a table or countertop and my computer

   B: A desk with storage drawers or shelves

   C: A separate room

4. **What kitchen appliances are a must? Choose all that apply.**

   A: Dishwasher

   B: Stovetop

   C: Oven

   D: Pressure cooker

   E: Stand mixer

   F: Microwave

5. **What can't you give up in your living space? Choose all that apply.**

   A: Bathtub

   B: Washer/dryer

   C: Walk-in closet

   D: Dining table for six

   E: Don't need any of the above

6. **Do both you and your significant other want to live tiny?**

   Yes, we both are excited about the possibility.

   No, I do, but my partner doesn't want to or is more hesitant.

7. **Are you willing to compromise on how your limited square footage will be used to meet your needs and your partner's needs?**

Yes

No

8. **How important is your privacy when living with others? Choose one.**

A: A must

B: It'd be nice to have a semi-separate space to retreat to.

C: That's what headphones are for.

9. **If you have a kid, what kind of bedroom do you want for yourself? Choose one. (Skip if not applicable.)**

A: An open-air loft

B: A loft with privacy screen

C: A downstairs bedroom with a partition

D: A downstairs bedroom with a door

FINANCES

1. **Do you have $10,000 to $30,000 available to put toward a self-build or purchase of a tiny house (down payment for a loan)? Choose one.**

A: Yes!

B: Not yet, but will in the next one to three years

C: No, and not likely to happen in the next five years

D: I have a few thousand saved up and plan to pay for the build in cash as I go.

2. Is your credit score 500 or above?

Yes

No

3. How much can you afford for housing every month? Choose one.

A: $300 or less

B: $300 to 800

C: $800 to 1000

PERSONALITY

1. Are you curious about new people, places, and experiences? Choose one.

A: Absolutely

B: Sort of

C: Not really

2. Does uncertainty cause you to be anxious? Choose one.

A: Rarely

B: Occasionally

C: Typically

D: Always

3. How much do you enjoy time alone? Choose one.

A: All-day, every day is my preference.

B: Alone time is a top priority, but I enjoy seeing others regularly.

C: I need social interaction daily or at least a couple of times a week.

Answer Key

Add up the points for every answer selected.

KNOW YOUR WHY

A: 2	**B**: 1	**C**: 4	**D**: 1	**E**: 2	**F**: 8
G: 1	**H**: 3	**I**: 2			

LIFESTYLE

1. Entertaining

A: 1   **B**: 4

2. Pets

A: 2   **B**: 2   **C**: 3   **D**: 4   **E**: 2   **F**: 2

3. Hobby storage

A: 1   **B**: 2   **C**: 3   **D**: 4

4. Outdoor recreation

A: 2   **B**: 2   **C**: 3   **D**: 2   **E**: 2

LOCATION

1. Neighbors

    A: 1   **B:** 2   **C:** 2   **D:** 5

2. Location flexibility

    A: 1   **B:** 2   **C:** 4   **D:** 7   **E:** 1

3. Move frequency

    A: 5   **B:** 1   **C:** 3   **D:** 3   **E:** 2

DOWNSIZING

1. Parting with belongings

    Yes: 1   **No:** 5

2. Storage unit

    Yes: 2   **No:** 1

3. Storage unit use

    A: 2   **B:** 8   **C:** 2

4. Keeping everything

    Yes: 8   **No:** 1

5. Sacrificing comforts

    Yes: 1   **No:** 8

LIVING NEEDS

1. **Inhabitants**

   A: 1   **B**: 2   **C**: 2   **D**: 3   **E**: 4   **F**: 6

2. **Work from home**

   Yes: 2   **No**: 1

3. **Office Space**

   A: 1   **B**: 2   **C**: 6

4. **Kitchen appliances**

   A: 6   **B**: 1   **C**: 2   **D**: 2   **E**: 6   **F**: 3

5. **Can't give up**

   A: 2   **B**: 2   **C**: 4   **D**: 8   **E**: 1

6. **Alignment**

   Yes: 1   **No**: 8

7. **Compromise**

   Yes: 1   **No**: 8

8. **Privacy**

   A: 4   **B**: 2   **C**: 1

9. **Bedroom privacy**

   A: 1   **B**: 2   **C**: 3   **D**: 4

FINANCES

1. Money available

    A:1   **B**: 2   **C**:8   **D**:4

2. Credit score

    Yes:1   **No**: 5

3. Monthly payment

    A: 4   **B**: 2   **C**:1

PERSONALITY

1. Curiosity

    A:1   **B**: 3   **C**:8

2. Uncertainty

    A:1   **B**: 2   **C**:4   **D**: 8

3. Alone time

    A: 6   **B**: 2   **C**:1

Score Analysis

35–71: TINY ALL THE WAY!

Tiny-house living is ideal for you right now or in the near future. You're open-minded, flexible, and ready to start downsizing. Because your needs are minimal and you likely don't have kids at home, a variety of tiny houses will work for you.

The kind of tiny house you choose, on wheels or a foundation, dictates how long the build process will take and the final price tag. Fortunately, you're financially flexible and down to go where the wind takes you, which means you'll have the maximum amount of permanent placement or parking options.

72–129: A SPECIFIC KIND OF TINY-HOUSE LIFE MAY BE RIGHT FOR YOU

A tiny house is in your future, but it may take two to five years to begin your build. To meet your particular needs, you should plan for a highly custom design and invest in one of the larger, more expensive tiny homes.

Downsizing won't be easy for you. It will likely be a slow, drawn-out process, but one that's well worth it. Your anxiety about the complexities and uncertainties involved in transitioning to a tiny house shouldn't deter you. It's complicated, and that's okay. Take your time, but keep pushing yourself to take the next step, even if it's one baby step after another.

You'll need to do quite a bit of legwork to find your ideal living arrangement. Based on your preferences, your placement or parking options will be more limited. Because of this, you'll likely need a higher-end monthly budget for housing expenses, whether it's a land payment or a lot lease in your desired community.

130-PLUS: TINY-HOUSE LIVING ISN'T A GREAT FIT FOR YOU RIGHT NOW

Tiny-house living is an enticing prospect, but it may not be the right fit for you—not right now, anyway. Do some soul-searching about your top goals and priorities and what you can start working on to inch closer to achieving them.

If a tiny house feels too limiting for you and your partner or family, a small traditional home might be a great way to downsize. If you decide to jump into tiny living, you probably want to build a house on your own land with outbuildings for additional storage. This will require a hefty up-front investment.

If you're single but actively looking for a committed living partner, consider adding extra space in your tiny-house design to accommodate them. Be prepared for a potentially uncomfortable conversation with a future significant other. They may not want to live tiny. If you both land on a different living arrangement, your investment in a tiny house can still be valuable! You can sell it, or turn it into a short-term rental for ongoing supplemental income.

If lack of funds is your primary obstacle, there are options. You can apply to tiny house grant programs created to make homeownership more accessible for those struggling financially. Additionally, a growing number of nonprofits are now developing permanently affordable tiny-home communities.

Note that the questionnaire is just a tool designed to help you ask yourself some important questions. It's not meant to tell you what you can or cannot do. Check out the Resources at the back of the book (page 125) for more information on determining your needs.

Relationships

When it comes to living tiny with others, your patience will be tested. That's just the nature of sharing 400 square feet or less.

In a larger house it can be easy to avoid conflict, with each party retreating to separate rooms. There's no room for running away from problems in a tiny house. Your communication skills can make or break your relationship with a significant other.

Identifying each party's needs is important, both before and after moving in, to minimize frustration. Things as simple as agreeing on how much storage space each person gets goes a long way in feeling satisfied. Establishing daily routines is also essential for preventing unnecessary conflict, like who gets ready in the bathroom first.

There's no avoiding the fact that you will get in each other's way sometimes. But with a little patience and kindness, a peaceful household is possible in a tiny house.

A productive side effect of living tiny together is becoming better acquainted with each other's communication styles. Overall, the amount of verbal and nonverbal communication dramatically increases when a couple or family shares a small space. This can help fine-tune your perception of your loved one's emotional signals, needs, and quirks. Understanding each other better leads to improved communication and builds trust.

While the tiny-house lifestyle can help strengthen your relationships, it's best to go into it with a substantial level of established trust and commitment to help you work through problems together. Otherwise, the increased pressure of small-space living could result in irreparable damage.

As you consider taking the tiny plunge together, ask yourself the hard questions about your relationship. How stable is your foundation? Do you see a significant lifestyle change as a band-aid for any problems in your relationship? Tiny-house living will only exacerbate existing issues.

PRIVACY

Downsizing into a tiny house also drastically reduces privacy. An open floor plan maximizes usable space. Naturally, that translates into almost no interior doors or truly separate rooms, though there are exceptions.

If you're single, the only privacy concern is from the outside world, which can be easily addressed with window coverings. For couples or families, limited privacy will be your everyday experience. For instance, the bathroom is never far away. Get comfortable with someone else using it in close proximity. Exhaust fans can minimize odor, but they can be noisy.

More importantly, are you someone who values or even depends on alone time to recharge your batteries? You'll want to consider your home's layout choices carefully. For example, a downstairs bedroom with a closing door, opposite of the living area, might be ideal.

Couples with fewer privacy concerns will have an easier go of it in various tiny home layouts. Believe it or not, you can get away from each other if you really want to, even in an extra-tiny space. Reading a book nestled back in our loft can feel like a separate room from the living area below. The mattress helps muffle sound transfer from downstairs. Privacy screens can also help. Headphones go a long way in creating privacy bubbles, even if you're only five feet away from your partner. Being alone together is a real thing. It's a simple way to respect each other's space without being physically distant.

However, there are practical needs that require privacy, like working from home, where you may need to make frequent calls or require complete concentration. If that's the case, you may want to invest in a larger model that allows for a separate home office with a door.

TINY-HOUSE LIVING WITH CHILDREN

While most tiny houses are best suited to one or two people, some can be customized to fit more occupants. In fact, many families prove that it can be done with multiple kids. But why would they want to?

For some families, it's about prioritizing togetherness. For others, it's about teaching their children the values of communication and environmentalism, and that living within your means can be fulfilling.

A tiny house can meet a growing family's needs with extra creativity and planning. While it requires some sacrifice, like less play space and limited storage for personal belongings, the limited interior space might result in more outdoor play—a healthy compromise.

Sharing a small space with kids can be challenging but creates opportunities to teach them valuable lessons and instill positive behaviors. It will require specific routines for activities, from sharing the bathroom to daily tidying. Every family member must help maintain order by cleaning up after themselves. Kids will learn to be conscious of resources like energy usage.

If you're considering moving into a tiny house with your kids, discuss each person's needs, desires, and feelings about it both as a family and one-on-one. When everyone feels heard, the downsizing process can lead to more thoughtful outcomes. But it might not be a good idea if a child feels overly anxious about this dramatic change. Families with more than two kids might want to avoid squeezing into 400 square feet or less. For example, fitting in more than two functional bedrooms typically isn't feasible.

Keep in mind that a child's needs shift over time. For instance, a tiny bedroom might work well for a young child, but it might be literally too small as they enter their teenage years. Teenagers also tend to value privacy more as they get older.

Editing Your Life

Downsizing is essential for transitioning into a tiny house. By deciding to live this way, you'll need to be comfortable with getting rid of as much as two-thirds of your belongings. Ultimately, it can end up being one of the most liberating experiences of your life. But preparing to downsize can feel daunting—and downright terrifying for some. This is because our stuff is more than just physical items. Much of it is loaded with emotional baggage.

Memories, good and bad, are often associated with our belongings. You might not even realize the extent of the emotional complexities until you start sorting through everything. Be prepared for a slow, thoughtful process; it will be hard to say goodbye to some of the things you own. Keep in mind, this process will help you distinguish between what's holding you back and what helps you live your life priorities. Through this experience, you can get better acquainted with yourself.

While drastically downsizing may be an unnerving prospect at first, that feeling is normal whenever you're making a significant change. We'll dive into the nitty-gritty on approaching this and break it down into manageable steps in chapter 7.

An essential component to editing your life is honestly and bravely facing yourself and thereby your collection of belongings. Don't let fear stand in the way of achieving a more fulfilling life, but don't rush the process either. The last thing you want to do is regret letting go of precious components of your life.

Everything in Its Place

Fact: Tiny houses get messier faster than bigger homes. The upside, of course, is that it doesn't take long to tidy up. This doesn't mean that big houses are cleaner or better organized. It's just easier to hide your stuff or disperse messiness when you have more space.

Sometimes, when you're busy, it's easy to lazily toss things on the couch or counter. Leaving stuff lying around for an extended amount of time can make your tiny home look extra unorganized and untidy. But more than that, it will feel chaotic, which is not the simplicity you seek when living tiny.

It only takes a few out-of-place items to make a tiny house feel cluttered or even claustrophobic. Do not underestimate the value of creating a place for everything. This helps you more easily return things to their "home" when you're done using them. This simple habit can keep your living space clean, tidy, and clutter-free—no matter how tiny your space.

A PROFILE IN TINY-HOUSE LIVING

Meet Shannen, a strong woman and mother to two boys and their English bulldog. She built her tiny house with her husband for about $45,000, and then they split up. Detangling their lives after 19 years together while trying to minimize the negative impact on their sons has been a challenge.

"This house has pretty much saved me. It's allowed me to get out from being with someone I couldn't be with any longer, and still be able to have my house and be able to have the boys come to a place they know and are comfortable in," Shannen explains. After separating, she moved her tiny house on wheels just 10 minutes away from her ex, providing a smoother transition for her and her boys.

Fortunately, Shannen's tiny house layout is spacious enough not to sacrifice family essentials like a small dining table, big sofa, and full-size bathtub—all ideal for two young boys. They have their own 8½-by-11-foot loft, which they can access via a curved metal ship ladder with a sturdy handrail. Homeschool takes place on the downstairs table that easily seats four. The storage stairs include a cubby dedicated to school supplies.

"The boys like the tiny house; they love their loft," Shannen says. "They are learning some good habits. We got rid of a lot of their stuff, but we let them choose the special things they kept."

The lifestyle change also cut down on relatives giving them stuff. "For birthdays, it's one small gift, and we do an experience. We go somewhere and do something. It's 'What do we get to do?' instead of 'What do I get?' So it's been a good transition."

Making It Work for You

Imagine saving hundreds and even thousands of dollars on monthly living expenses while saving countless hours spent cleaning your home. With a tiny house, the financial freedom and extra time are just some of the advantages you can enjoy.

While a tiny home can help you achieve your big goals, it isn't a silver bullet to solve all your problems. As you've seen, there are also realities that you should consider, like your living needs and how to downsize.

But if you're ready to embrace this lifestyle and its benefits, the challenges of transitioning to a tiny house could be minimal compared to the payoff of a more fulfilling and balanced life. If you don't mind getting creative, a tiny home could work for you, your significant other, and even a couple of kids in tow.

Now that you have a clear understanding of what it takes to live tiny, it's time to explore the diverse types of tiny houses available to you.

CHAPTER THREE

GOiNG MOBiLE: TiNY HOUSES ON WHEELS

Nothing quite captures one's imagination about downsized living like tiny homes on wheels. It speaks to the deep-seated wanderlust inside all of us, harkening back to our species' nomadic roots. A mobile dwelling is both practical and adventurous.

Although the freedom to pick up and travel with your cozy home whenever you want is a romantic notion, a majority of people who live in movable houses aren't full-time nomads. For most, mobility offers lifestyle flexibility and the ability to relocate when the need or desire arises. The ease and cost of relocation also vary greatly based on the kind of home you choose.

In this chapter, you'll learn more about the challenges of hitting the road and the differences between the various mobile tiny home options. Interested in creative conversions on wheels such as vans and buses? We'll get into those in chapter 5.

Types of Mobile Tiny Homes

Did you know mobile tiny homes have been around for thousands of years? A dwelling that could be moved from place to place was invented for convenience but also for sustenance, trade, and exploration. Mobility became an enduring way of life for some peoples.

As centuries have rolled forward, so has innovation around efficient mobile design. How do you fit a kitchen, bathroom, and sleeping space into a small roaming structure? And how can one secure breakable objects while in transit? Over the years, people have come up with creative solutions to deal with the unique challenges that come from living in a movable home.

Let's dig into the four major categories of mobile tiny homes, from the road-trip-ready to floating abodes.

RVS

Recreational vehicles have a long, rich history in the United States. In fact, the first professionally manufactured RV and camper trailers debuted way back in 1910 and became popular as a practical way to travel. And as early as the Great Depression, they were seen as a way to live affordably when the economy made homeownership difficult. The term "RV" refers to a wide variety of recreational vehicles, including motorhomes with engines, travel trailers towed behind your vehicle, truck campers that sit in the bed of a truck, and more.

The use of RVs as year-round homes has grown immensely, since the mid-20th century and into the present day, for those seeking a significant lifestyle change. As of this book's writing, more than 1 million

Americans live in RVs full-time. While these people come from a broad range of socioeconomic backgrounds, the freedom to travel is a common motivator. But travel expenses can add up quickly, so those looking for a budget-friendly home tend to stay put. When considering going mobile full-time, carefully review available options and downsides before committing.

Towables

Travel trailers range from itty-bitty teardrops to beefy toy haulers. Neither of these specific options are ideal as full-time homes because of their limited living space. Fortunately, there's a wide array of other styles, floor plans, and price points to choose from, ranging between 10 to 40 feet in length.

Larger travel trailers, for example, have room for most necessary home functions and can be quite spacious. Slide-out models create significantly wider room sizes, often for the kitchen, dining area, or bedroom. On the whole, fifth-wheels are the largest towable RV option—extending over the bed of a truck. Top benefits include exceptional storage space and increased towing maneuverability.

Depending on travel trailer weight, the necessary tow vehicle can range from a midsize SUV to a heavy-duty pickup truck.

Motorhomes

With motorhomes, you don't need to worry about tow vehicles, but the price tag is much higher. You can choose from three types. Class A is the largest and most expensive category, with its cost averaging between $80,000 and $200,000. Think of these as mobile luxury apartments. Class B is for zippy, compact campervans. Lastly, Class C is the midsize, least expensive motorhome category.

Advantages and Disadvantages

RVs are tried-and-true homes on wheels. You can enjoy a roomy living space that can be easily moved from place to place. However, many options are not suitable for four-season living due to poor insulation and energy inefficiency. Most importantly, RVs do not have lasting durability due to flimsy materials used inside and out. You also pay big if you want to enjoy extra space, premium features, and higher-quality insulation. Upkeep costs can also set you back several hundred dollars, or more, per year. While used RVs can be reasonably inexpensive, they often need much work. But custom renovations on both used or new RVs can be well worth it to significantly improve overall aesthetics and interior durability. Finally, RV parking options are expansive. But beware of the 10-year rule; some RV parks bar older models because of weathered or dingy appearance.

TINY HOUSES ON WHEELS

As discussed in chapter 1, tiny houses on wheels (THOW) are a hybrid between RV features and residential construction quality. They rose to popularity as a more affordable way to create a simple custom home not available on the housing market. The diversity of THOW designs is as great as the number of people living in them.

The ability to customize a tiny house on wheels is perhaps its biggest benefit. You can tailor your design specifically for your style, needs, and lifestyle preferences. Building your own THOW is the most affordable option, especially for custom features, as you'll see in chapter 6.

Tiny houses on wheels are built on either bumper pull or fifth-wheel trailers, typically between 16 and 40 feet long. You can choose between the standard road-ready 8½-foot-wide or 10- to 12-foot-wide sizes. Tiny houses on wheels are as tall as a Class A RV, typically 13½ feet with an interior height of 10½ feet. You can maximize your limited square footage by adding lofts for sleeping and additional storage.

Whether you prefer a sleek, modern look or a craftsman-style bungalow feel, you can achieve the style you want with a tiny house on wheels. The same is true for the interior, because you can work with the full range of residential finishes and materials. Certain design choices, like sheetrock and marble countertops, affect the overall weight, which is vital to track when building on a movable foundation.

Finding a THOW design that will work for you can be a complicated process. Touring tiny homes is an excellent way to review different layouts and design features. While YouTube can be a great resource, in-person tours are ideal for experiencing the space firsthand and identifying what resonates with you. Tiny living festivals offer a wide variety of homes in one convenient place. Or book a few nights at different tiny house Airbnbs, if you can. Be mindful that it's easy to get dazzled by all the cuteness; be sure to look for mundane but crucial features like clothing storage. Take notes, too!

Compiling a list of your wants versus needs is paramount when you're planning to move into a tiny house on wheels. This also helps you understand what's essential in your living space and what you need to achieve your lifestyle goals. See chapter 7 for an in-depth downsizing guide.

VARDOS

Homes on wheels first appeared in Europe in the early 19th century. Vardos, also known as living wagons or caravans, were originally used by traveling circuses and later adopted by the Roma people. As nomadic people, they would travel from place to place for seasonal work or to escape persecution. That's what made their wooden horse-drawn wagons, used as living quarters, so practical. Their colorful vardos were often ornately decorated with carvings and intricate paintings, and sometimes even gilded. More lavish and elaborate designs signified the economic status of wealthy Romani families. Building one took 6 to 12 months by commissioned custom craftspeople. Once completed, a 10- to 13-foot-long caravan was typically gifted to a newlywed couple.

Over time, six primary vardo styles have developed: Bowtop, Burton, Brush Wagon, Ledge, Openlot, and Reading. Each kind features tremendous craftsmanship and distinctive characteristics reflective of the lifestyle of its owners. Caravans were always known as cozy and warm houses on wheels. Every caravan included a wood stove for heating and cooking. All were outfitted with built-in seating, cabinetry, and sleeping bunks. Parents slept in the larger upper bed; children slept in the bottom bunk.

There's been a revival in vardo building for glamping accommodations and tiny homes in recent years from both DIYers and custom building companies. Instead of requiring horses, these contemporary vardos have been fashioned into small towable trailers that can be pulled by automobiles or trucks. Larger models incorporate small refrigerators, kitchen sinks, and micro-bathrooms to accommodate full-time use. But many stay true to original caravans, featuring artistic designs and curved roofs.

Fun fact: Modern travel trailers are referred to as caravans in Europe, South Africa, Australia, and New Zealand.

HOUSEBOATS

People have lived on boats for hundreds of years, especially for long voyages. Now around the world, hundreds of thousands call liveaboard boats "home." A liveaboard boat is simply a vessel that a person makes their primary residence. It can be anything from a yacht to a sailboat to a houseboat. The allure of life on the water is appealing to many with a strong case of wanderlust. Home can be anywhere you anchor it. Whereas for others, it's more about affordable living that often comes with million-dollar waterfront views.

Houseboats are designed primarily for use as floating dwellings, so less emphasis is placed on the efficiency of its function as a boat. Instead, creature comforts are prioritized. They range in size from 200 to over 1000 square feet, often in a two-story layout—though most are 400 to 600 square feet. The average cost of a houseboat is approximately $50,000. As with other homes, the larger the size, the more expensive the cost.

Houseboats come in three general categories. The primary difference is the level of mobility.

Bluewater or cruising houseboats feature an engine or sails to propel them. These can be more easily relocated, and importantly, can be taken on open-water excursions. Further, bluewater houseboats have more off-grid capability, ideal for mooring in bays with no utility hookups.

Non-cruising houseboats are primarily stationary and harbored with limited mobile capacity. Some have a tiny engine or sail, while others only move when towed by another vessel.

Floating homes are completely stationary. They permanently float in a waterway, connected to shore-based utilities year-round. Unlike the other houseboat categories, floating homes most resemble traditional houses. Styles range widely: ultra-modern, cottage-style, or quirky cabins. Floating homes tend to rock less than other houseboats, which means less chance of getting seasick.

Weight distribution can be a concern when it comes to appliance and furniture placement. The interior layout is easy on one hand because floating homes use a flat flooring system like a regular house—in contrast to the slightly curved hull of other houseboats. But if weight is unevenly distributed, the house will list and require flotation adjustments under the home.

Living in a houseboat comes with the joys of a greater connection to nature. Whether you take trips or stay put, wildlife sightings are common, like seabirds, seals, and whales. Also, you can enjoy neighborly community life with others choosing to live alternatively. Marinas offer long-term docking leases, and European canals have long-term mooring sites. Similarly, you can join a floating home community in many countries. Fees can be as low as a few hundred dollars or as high as $1,000 per month. Keep in mind that laws and rules vary.

Available houseboat financing options depend on the type. Most lenders tend to consider mobile versions like RVs, though floating homes can qualify for shorter-term mortgages. Overall, houseboat life offers significant savings compared to typical homeownership. But like a car, you need to plan for regular inspections and maintenance such as mechanical tune-ups and hiring a diving service to clean the bottom of your boat. Specialized repairs are pricey. Marine mechanics, for instance, can charges as much as $100 per hour.

Zoning and the THOW

When considering a tiny house on wheels, the biggest question is always, "Where can I park?" The uncertainty and anxiety around parking keeps many people from pursuing the idea any further.

As longtime nomadic tiny-house dwellers, we experienced more parking flexibility than most full-timers. We've stayed in a wide array of locales, from rural to urban, and in backyards, campgrounds, or at RV-friendly businesses. Often, we parked in tiny-home communities or even formed our own temporary "micro-hood" with other nomadic dwellers. Typically, our stays corresponded with allowed overnight to two-week-long stays. Other times we didn't follow any rules but weren't concerned because of the short length of our visit.

For long-term parking, there are more options available than you may realize. But legwork is often required to find your ideal spot. It's important to note that most cities don't have legal avenues for tiny-house parking due to restrictive zoning. Zoning laws regulate how land is developed, including what kinds of structures are allowed.

If you want hassle-free parking, go where it's already allowed. By that, we mean places that are approved for full-time living or extended stays, such as in tiny-home communities or cities with tiny-friendly zoning. While RV parks and campgrounds are more readily available, they can have stay restrictions—14 days to three seasons only.

An ever-growing number of cities recognize the value of THOWs as infill housing, specifically as accessory dwelling units (ADUs). THOWs can rapidly increase housing supply, like a kind of instant development that uses existing land and infrastructure. This all translates into reduced costs, resources, and impact.

A THOW accessory dwelling unit means parking on a property with a primary residence. It's a practical and convenient situation and typically near resources like shopping. Backyard parking is mutually beneficial for the tiny dweller and property owner. Lot lease can go toward paying the mortgage and taxes, and maintaining the property. This has proven to be valuable for single parents, elderly homeowners, or anyone who needs extra help. How much you pay for your backyard spot is negotiated by the landowner and tiny dweller—typically $200 to $700 per month inclusive of utilities. Sometimes work-for-trade arrangements are established. For example, the THOW dweller may be responsible for some maintenance duties, like shoveling snow, in exchange for reduced rent.

In big and small cities where THOW accessory dwelling units are allowed, you'll need to apply for a permit and meet specific requirements. For instance, your THOW must be certified to meet basic building standards. Second, it must be connected to city utilities. Additionally, the undercarriage (wheels, axles, etc.) must be skirted.

Do you dream of parking your THOW on your own land? Opportunities to do this legally are rare. Most commonly, this is available in rural settings with no zoning. But other regulations exist for sanitation and water runoff.

Numerous North American cities now have zoning laws allowing tiny houses on wheels primarily as ADUs and in community settings. But tens of thousands more municipalities are left. Demand in other countries, like Australia and New Zealand, is growing as well.

For now, most THOW dwellers live in legal communities. Or they're parked, under the radar, in backyards at the mercy of their neighbors. One neighbor complaint can result in a code violation notice and eviction in as little as 48 hours or up to 90 days. If you are uncomfortable with risk, choose to park in an existing legal locale. You can also join tiny-home organizations advocating for more legal permanent placement options to help create change in your preferred location.

For a deep dive into these topics, see the Advocacy and Parking sections in the Resources at the back of the book (pages 133 and 132).

A PROFILE IN TINY-HOUSE LIVING

Meet Marek and Kothney-Issa, proud Millennial tiny homeowners. They went from a large downtown loft apartment to a 204-square-foot tiny house on wheels. Downsizing, for them, didn't mean sacrificing comfort or function. But it required careful layout consideration with their builder. For six-foot-five Marek, a tall-friendly design was essential.

Their tiny-house design efficiently achieves their creature comfort wish list. Impressively, it features a king-size bed, 55-inch TV, stackable washer/dryer, and his-and-her closets. Kothney-Issa shares, "My favorite part of the tiny home is definitely the kitchen. I'm super excited that we're in a tiny home and still have counter space. We have a whole section I never use."

As Marek puts it, the tiny house feels even more comfortable because it's theirs. "Something about ownership feels different than renting. Just to be able to own this and be able to pay for it in a reasonable amount of time is freeing for us. It's new for us. It's small, but it's ours." Achieving their financial goals was a top motivation for downsizing. By dramatically reducing their monthly expenses and working multiple jobs, they are now completely debt-free. They paid off $125,000 in a mere two years.

During this time, a new job opportunity came up for Marek. This led them to relocate from an RV park in Florida to a tiny-home village in Texas. But just a year after settling in, Marek and Kothney-Issa received huge news: They're expecting their first baby! They then decided to hit the road with their tiny house on wheels to be near family in their hometown of Kansas City. With debt gone and a new home base secure, this enterprising couple is now exploring investment possibilities for their future. Their next financial challenge: developing their own tiny-house community!

What You Need to Know to Hit the Road

We have traveled more than 55,000 miles with our tiny house on wheels. Over four and a half years, we towed our home to 36 states and one Canadian province. Consequently, our THOW has been through the desert, to both coasts, and over 10,000 feet above sea level. Tiny-house travel hasn't always been an easy experience. The most important lessons we learned were what not to do, like never leave without two spare tires and wheels.

Whether you're a full-time nomad or just relocating to a new city, preparation is essential before hitting the road with your tiny home on wheels.

STATE AND FEDERAL HIGHWAY LAWS

Every kind of home on wheels you plan to tow or drive must comply with federal and state laws. These laws dictate size, weight, equipment requirements, and other safety factors you need to consider while navigating highways and the interstate system. In most U.S. states, the maximum RV/THOW size is 13½ feet tall and 8½ feet wide. The maximum length for motorhomes is 45 feet, but for towable trailers, it varies between 53 and 65 feet, including your tow vehicle. You can go wider with an inexpensive wide-load permit. But once you exceed 12 or 14 feet, in most states, there are more costly requirements, like the use of escort vehicles. If you want to go taller or longer, you'll need expensive special permits and professional movers.

When choosing your width and length, you need to consider where you want to take your THOW. Is it for road-tripping or a more permanent parking spot? If you want to visit National Parks, for instance, you'll want your total length to be 27 feet or less to meet restrictions for the greatest number of parks. Of course, for larger THOWs, you can always stay at an RV park nearby and drive your tow vehicle in.

Most THOWs do not require a special driver's license unless it's over 26,000 pounds. If it's over that weight, 17 states require either a commercial driver's license (CDL) or a special non-commercial license. Check with your state's motor vehicle agency for specifics. You always want to meet your home state's licensing requirements. If you do this, you will not get into trouble in other U.S. states or Canadian provinces.

Many states require that trailers be equipped with safety features like trailer lights and breakaway brake systems. Even if not required, it's in your best interest to have these. A breakaway system will activate your trailer's brakes if it becomes disconnected from the tow vehicle.

The good news is that if you comply with these regulations, you can travel with your THOW across the highway system without any issues as long as you obey all posted signs and speed limits. Keep in mind that RVs must remain in the right lane, except when passing, preparing to turn, or entering or exiting the highway.

Bridge clearances and gross-weight limits can happen on smaller roads. When planning your route through scenic byways or other side roads, you'll need to be aware of challenges like steep grades, ultra-low bridges and tunnels, and propane restrictions for some tunnels. There are many route-planning tools online to help you navigate these issues.

CHOOSING TRAILERS AND HITCHES

When the time comes to hitch up your home on wheels and hit the road, you need the proper gear. You'll need a complete hitch system composed of the tow vehicle, trailer, and the equipment used to connect them—most important, the trailer hitch.

Choosing a trailer for your tiny house on wheels is one of the most critical decisions you'll make. It's your foundation and what enables you to move from place to place. The style of trailer you choose also affects the look, layout, and maneuverability of your tiny house. So, you need to select your trailer before your tiny house can be designed and built.

Used Trailers

Buying a used trailer seems enticing because it is less expensive than a new trailer. But, simply put, the initial savings isn't worth it. Any used option, a utility or RV trailer, is risky. You'll need to modify a used trailer to be able to build your tiny house onto it. Plan on hiring a welder, unless you happen to be one. Failing to identify weakness in the trailer, skimping on upgrades, or being unaware of the weight capacity can lead to significant issues down the road, translating into hefty expenses.

That said, repurposing used trailers safely is possible. The most important thing to look for when shopping for a used trailer is a weight rating placard to confirm that both the frame and axles can support the weight of your tiny house. Without this essential information, you have no clear way of knowing. Refurbishing a used RV trailer for a THOW may seem like a no-brainer, but keep in mind that RV construction uses significantly lighter materials than the standard tiny house and isn't designed to support the same weight. Using a steel framing THOW kit is likely the best way to go, but then again, you'll need professional help and customization to pull this off successfully. A steel framing kit is made from machine-manufactured lightweight yet durable galvanized steel—a DIY-friendly option for tiny houses on wheels and on foundations.

Specialized Tiny-House Trailers

The most secure option is to shop from specialist tiny-house trailer manufacturers. You can choose from standard sizes or commission a custom trailer to precisely match your unique plans. Tiny house–specific trailers are designed for safety and to be build-ready. Heavy-duty axles provide ample weight capacity for your structure. Most important, they feature secure steel connection points between the trailer and house to ensure they stay bonded together. An electric brake system is always included as well. Some manufacturers offer drop axles to maximize interior height, which allows several extra inches of headroom in sleeping lofts.

All of these tiny house trailer benefits equate to a substantial cost. Be prepared to spend $3,000 to $9,000, depending on the size.

Bumper Pull Trailers

A bumper pull trailer attaches to a ball hitch on the back bumper of a tow vehicle. Bumper pulls, in general, are the most common THOW trailer choice.

Bumper pulls allow you to build on a long, flat foundation, which results in a more traditional house-like appearance. They are available as dual or triple axle trailers depending on your needs. Tri-axles are used for longer, heavier tiny houses. Bumper pulls also provide the greatest number of tow vehicle options, ranging from SUVs to a variety of trucks.

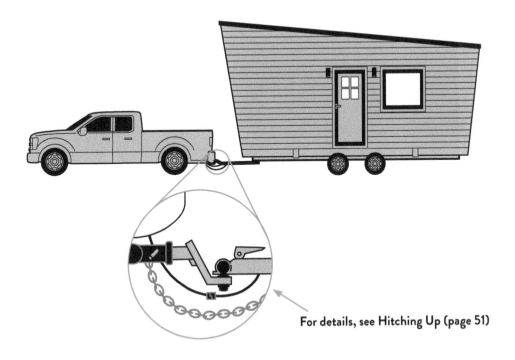

For details, see Hitching Up (page 51)

Gooseneck/Fifth-Wheel Trailers

Like fifth-wheel travel trailers, a gooseneck trailer attaches to a mount in the bed of your truck. Gooseneck trailers provide additional space and towing stability, making this a popular choice for many tiny house owners. It's also somewhat less expensive than a fifth-wheel.

The difference between a fifth-wheel and a gooseneck is how it connects to the pickup truck; a fifth-wheel attaches via a hinged plate hitch, while a gooseneck slides onto a ball hitch. The main advantage of a gooseneck hitch is its slim profile. Both offer a smoother tow experience with greater maneuverability and stability than a bumper pull. Additionally, both distribute the THOW's tongue weight mainly over the truck's rear axle instead of the trailer frame's back, like with a bumper pull. As a result, sway is minimized and you can handle towing more weight. You can also make shaper turns, which helps you get into tighter parking spots.

Another top benefit is the ability to build over the arm of the gooseneck, the space over the hitch. This allows you to build a longer THOW without eating into your maximum length limit—because it goes over the truck bed. Use the extra space for utility closet storage and a full-height bedroom—not possible in a sleeping loft!

The primary disadvantage of a gooseneck trailer is that you're limited in tow-vehicle options: heavy-duty pickup trucks only. You'll need to own your own pickup or will need to hire out for hauling. Renting box trucks for occasional moves is out of the question.

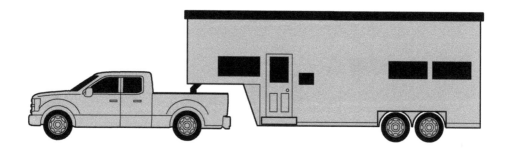

Hitching Up

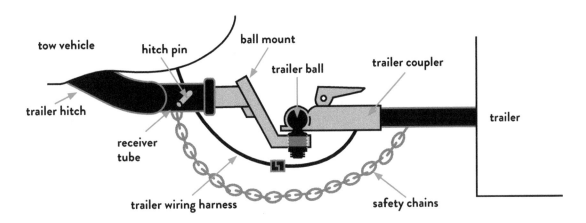

Once you've decided on a trailer, you need to install the correct corresponding hitch system. Gooseneck and fifth-wheel trailers use truck bed–mounted systems. A ball and coupler connection is used for goosenecks, similar to bumper pulls. In contrast, a fifth-wheel hitch uses a kingpin and pin receiver.

A bumper pull trailer hitch requires a receiver of some kind—an open receptacle on or below the bumper of the truck. Most quarter-ton to one-ton pickup trucks come with a receiver. If your tow vehicle doesn't come with one, a hitch receiver can be bolted or welded onto the chassis of the vehicle. A ball mount with an attached trailer ball inserts into the receiver.

Next, the trailer coupler attaches to the trailer ball. A coupler fits securely over the installed $2\frac{5}{16}$-inch ball, in most cases. All these components get securely locked into place. Importantly, most tiny house trailers come with a $2\frac{5}{16}$-inch trailer coupler. If you're not sure what size you have, check with your trailer manufacturer.

Installing a gooseneck or fifth-wheel hitch system is much more involved, and placement needs to be exact. So, as a beginner, you are better off hiring a professional to do this for you.

DOES YOUR VEHICLE HAVE WHAT IT TAKES?

Just because a vehicle can tow doesn't mean it can safely tow your tiny house on wheels! To tow your THOW, you need to purchase an SUV or truck that's up to the task. Towing capacity, or the maximum amount of trailer weight a vehicle can tow, is the important factor to consider. Exceeding this amount will put unnecessary stress on your vehicle's engine and could damage the rear axle and transmission. Engine size, horsepower, and torque are also vital aspects of towing capacity.

Before you begin your search, you need to know your THOW's weight. A 5,000-pound vardo and a 14,000-pound tiny house require much different towing capacity. You want to know the gross trailer weight (GTW), the trailer's total weight, plus its cargo. That means a fully loaded THOW with appliances, clothing, and everything. Only the lightest THOW can be towed by an SUV or lightweight half-ton pickup truck. Most need a heavy-duty, one- to three-quarter-ton truck.

Fortunately, maximum towing capacity of most truck models is readily available from the manufacturer and via several online calculators. Keep in mind, you want a vehicle whose capacity is 3,000 to 5,000 pounds more than your THOW's weight to avoid overly stressing your truck's engine. For example, if your THOW's gross trailer weight is 12,000 pounds, you want to choose a truck that can tow at least 15,000 pounds. Also, the higher the capacity, the more leeway you have for any extra weight you may add during future renovations.

Manufacturers often offer towing packages with a trailer wiring harness, electric trailer brakes, and upgraded suspension components. Spending a little extra on this is very worthwhile, especially as it relates to the braking system. If your truck doesn't come with an integrated brake controller system, you must purchase one and have it installed. A working trailer braking system connected to your tow vehicle is absolutely crucial for towing safety. Hitting the brakes in the truck activates the trailer brakes. As a result, both slow down at the same controlled pace. Without trailer brakes, slowing down is more difficult and takes longer.

TOWING

Just because your house has wheels does not mean it is road-trip ready. It is very appealing to think you can take it almost anywhere. But if your dream tiny home needs a triple axle trailer, it is most likely not intended for frequent relocation. Of course, that doesn't mean it can't be moved. Larger and heavier THOWs are more challenging to maneuver on the road and not well-suited for the inexperienced or faint of heart.

Travel prep begins during the design/build phase. Your tiny-house design needs to reflect how often you plan to move. The bigger and heavier the THOW, the more difficult it is to tow. For frequent moving, smaller and lighter is the way to go. No matter the final size, overall weight distribution is critical for a safe tow experience. An unbalanced trailer can result in swerving on the road. Note that an anti-sway bar system, commonly used for travel trailers, will not fix poor distribution!

A good rule of thumb is the 60/40 split. Place 60 percent of the total tiny house weight in front of the axle (toward the tongue), and 40 percent behind. Also, ideally, your tongue weight should be 10 to 15 percent of your total THOW weight. Tongue weight is the downward force that the trailer tongue exerts on the hitch connection with your tow vehicle. Too much tongue weight can overload the truck's suspension and transmission, while too little will cause the trailer to sway uncontrollably. At the very least, this will result in an uncomfortable ride, but it could cause you to lose control of the THOW and crash. The easiest way to measure your tongue weight during the build is with a tongue weight scale.

Your Tow Prep List

Always check your tow prep list twice before getting on the road. When it comes to traveling with a THOW, you can never be too careful. Properly hooking up your trailer to the tow vehicle involves many critical steps. Missing one can result in a catastrophe. Every single time you are ready to hit the road, go through your tow safety checklist:

☐ Proper tire pressure

☐ Secure attachment to the truck, including hitch lock and emergency breakaway system

☐ Working trailer brakes

☐ Working trailer lights

☐ Correct mirror placement

Driving Tips

Stay calm at all times. Think about towing your tiny house like a form of meditation. Your goal is to focus entirely on driving with precision. Stress and distractions may occur. That's okay. Traveling with a partner can help minimize these stressors. Your copilot can help navigate, put on your favorite podcast, and hand you a drink.

To stay focused while driving, ground yourself in the repetition of safe driving practices:

☐ Check your mirrors frequently.

☐ Change lanes gradually; never jerk the wheel.

☐ Take slow, wide turns.

☐ No matter what, don't rush. You'll get there when you get there, and probably late.

Expect the Unexpected

Towing misadventures happen. Like the time we got a flat tire on the way to Burning Man, or the time a wheel seized up and we had to limp it to a repair shop. What's remarkable about both mishaps is the kindness of strangers we experienced. A stranger offered help to fix the tire, and the shop allowed us to sleep in the tiny house overnight and even gave us power.

The delightful thing about having your home with you is that you can go inside to make coffee while you wait for a mobile repairman. That's precisely what we did when our rental truck got a flat tire. The more you travel with your THOW, the more likely you will find yourself in a temporary bind. Stay calm and trust that you will find a solution. However, you want to be prepared for when things go wrong. Always bring the following:

- ☐ Spare tire and wheel set
- ☐ One 12,000-pound jack (or more depending on the weight of house)
- ☐ Tire iron to remove lug nuts
- ☐ Jack stands/stabilizers
- ☐ Wheel levers

Remember, if you are not confident that you can tow your tiny home by yourself, hire an experienced hauling company to do it for you! And see the Resources section at the back of the book for towing how-to guides.

CHAPTER FOUR

STAYiNG PUT WiTH YOUR TiNY HOUSE

Whenever a "tiny house" is mentioned, people tend to think of one on wheels. But many tiny houses are not on wheels at all. Stationary tiny houses come in all kinds of shapes, and often they're referred to by their style, like cabin or cottage, instead of by their size.

Ground-bound tiny houses open the doors to another level of sustainable, self-reliant living. Whether on an itty-bitty parcel or a few acres, you can maximize your available outdoor space in an environmentally friendly way. Consider the possibilities of creating a homestead-like oasis with a robust garden and large-scale off-grid utilities, including rainwater catchment.

Ultimately, you can build a deeper connection to your surroundings when you're staying put. But being tied to the land comes with its own challenges, from zoning to caretaking necessities. Tiny-home communities offer practical solutions to some of these issues.

In this chapter, you'll learn all about the options, benefits, and realities of putting down roots with a tiny home.

Types of Stationary Tiny Houses

If you want the stability of a ground-bound home, you can choose from two main types of stationary tiny houses, built on either a temporary or permanent foundation.

Stationary doesn't have to mean immobile. That may seem odd, but it's true. Technically, any structure can be relocated. Have you seen videos of giant historic houses being moved? Accomplishing this feat can be pretty complicated and expensive, as you might imagine. While house moving is an infeasible proposition for most homeowners, tiny houses are much more practical to move via skids.

Permanent foundation–based tiny houses, however, provide more possibilities in design. Which foundation type is right for you?

TINY HOUSES ON FOUNDATIONS (THOF)

Unlike a tiny house on wheels, you can enjoy greater design freedom with a tiny house on a permanent foundation because it isn't restricted by height, length, or width. Choose from various permanent foundation systems, like concrete slab, crawlspace, or a pier foundation system. But there's a catch: You must own land. In a few cases, a long-term land lease is possible, like with a home on piers.

Concrete slab is the cheapest foundation to build because of the minimal labor required. It can be poured and dried in less than a day. Keep in mind, it is best suited for warmer climates. Freezing temps can cause the foundation to crack, creating structural instability. On the upside, concrete slabs prevent mold buildup, as well as rodent and insect infestation.

A crawlspace foundation, on the other hand, comes with a greater cost but more perks. It's essentially a shallow basement, a few feet off the ground. The under-house space gives the structure some air to breathe and room to store and access your utility systems. Compared to concrete, you can enjoy warmer floors with an adequately insulated crawlspace, making your home warmer as well. Another benefit is that it provides space to shelter you in extreme weather conditions, making it well-suited for tornado-prone areas.

A pier foundation, or post and beam, creates similar benefits to a crawl-space but at less cost. Its wooden beams sit on top of reinforced concrete footers buried into the ground. The beams support the house, and the entire foundation system raises it about 18 inches off the ground. A pier foundation system is ideal for a house built on sloped or flood-prone land.

You can realistically relocate a tiny house set on a pier foundation by hiring house movers. It's an involved and pricey process, with moves costing between $6,500 and $30,000 or more, depending on distance and other factors.

Tiny houses on foundations give you easier access to traditional financing opportunities. A stationary home is considered "real property," which refers to the land you own and any structures permanently attached to it. Lenders view them as ordinary houses, unlike tiny houses on wheels, which are classified as personal property.

The overall value of your tiny house on foundation will appreciate over time, providing an investment opportunity. But you need to anticipate double or even quadrupled up-front costs when building a permanently placed home. Unless you're already a landowner, you need to budget for the land purchase, along with infrastructure expenses, utility hookup fees, and permitting costs.

TINY HOUSES ON SKIDS

Building a tiny house on a temporary foundation gives you the option to move it relatively easily. A skid system uses two or more pressure-treated beams that support the floor structure. It's meant to be portable and is not permanently attached to the ground.

Skids act like sled rails, allowing you to drag the structure around using chains and a pickup truck. This is especially helpful if you want to reposition your tiny home on the same property. You can also load a tiny house on skids (THOS) onto a heavy-duty trailer to relocate it to an entirely new location. Using car jacks, simply jack the tiny house on skids up to slide it onto the trailer. (Detailed how-tos are available online.) Then you must carefully tie it down to ensure safe transport. You can haul it without permits, as long as it meets Department of Transportation overall size requirements, as laid out in chapter 3. During transport, the distance from the ground to the peak of your tiny house on skids counts toward the overall 13½-foot height restriction. The trailers typically used for hauling heavy loads have a significantly higher trailer bed than a specialized tiny-house trailer. Because of this, you lose 1½ to 5 feet of interior height in a THOS compared to a THOW.

One significant benefit of a tiny house on skids is the cost savings. You can save thousands on your build by skipping a tiny house on wheels trailer. But buying your own heavy-duty trailer to transport your tiny house on skids defeats that purpose. So, this is best for infrequent moves by a professional hauler. An average move cost within 50 miles is approximately $250 to $600. Add $1 to $3 per mile for farther distances.

Note that a tiny house on skids is considered a temporary structure, like a shed. Temporary structures don't have to meet the same stringent building codes or zoning rules, but are not intended to be used as a dwelling. Consequently, just like an unpermitted tiny house on wheels, one neighbor complaint can lead to eviction.

A PROFILE IN TINY-HOUSE LIVING

Meet Sol, a tiny homeowner living at the Port Townsend Ecovillage in Washington. As part of the intentional community, all the residents share resources, costs, and land maintenance tasks. "Anytime I want, I can walk out and talk to somebody, go to a garden party or work party or dance parties they have, and be social," she says. This is a big part of what Sol most loves about living here.

The Ecovillage is made up of numerous residential lots connected by greenspace. On one of the 4,000-square-foot lots, long-time village residents decided to develop a tiny-home lot to help more people afford to be a part of their community, like Sol, who is facing retirement on a fixed income. Now three legally permitted tiny houses, built to residential code standards, can be placed here.

Sol's 12-foot-wide, 400-square-foot tiny house is built on a pier foundation. The village charges the tiny-home residents an affordable lot lease partially based on the fact the houses can be relocated. "Technically, the house can be moved. Practically, it'd probably be $10-, $15-, $20,000 to move the house," she says. So Sol is exploring the financial benefits of buying her small lot instead of leasing the land.

Before going tiny, Sol owned a small house and sold it as part her downsizing plan to save money for retirement. From the sale, she made $100,000 in profit to put toward her tiny house on foundation, which she hoped to build for only $50,000. But to her surprise, it ended up costing double that due to unanticipated infrastructure costs. Sol explains that $17,000 had gone into the project before the builder stepped on the property. Utility hookup fees, permitting, and foundation-system costs add up quickly!

Styles of Stationary Tiny Houses

Perhaps the best thing about stationary tiny houses is the incredible design flexibility. You don't face the same precise size and rectangular shape limitations of building on wheels. You have more designs to choose from and more control over your floor plan. What shape most speaks to you? Choose a square, triangle, or round living space. Not a fan of crawl-in lofts? Build a full two-story. It's all about what suits your preferences and design aesthetic the best. Let's dive into six cozy, ground-bound tiny house styles.

CABINS

When you imagine a cabin, does imagery of the American frontier come to mind? Log cabins popped up wherever European immigrants spread across North America. It all began around 1638 when Swedish settlers built the first log cabins in the New World. The ingenious building technique of stacking and interlacing logs, without the need for nails and fancy tools, made them ideal homes for settlers with limited resources. Chinking was added to seal the space between the logs—a blend of available materials like clay, sand, and mud.

Early frontier-style cabins were only 120 to 200 square feet with one room, a stone fireplace, no windows, and sometimes a sleeping loft. Later, windows popped up to meet the requirements laid out in the 1862 U.S. Homestead Act. It gave "homesteaders" rights to claim open land but required that they cultivate it and build homes at least 10 by 12 feet in size, with at least one glass window. Over time, cabin designs evolved and expanded. Covered front porches became a common characteristic.

The rustic simplicity of log cabins continues to have appeal today. Modern tiny cabin design is incredibly similar to its simply designed forbearers. Cabin architecture has evolved into various styles, but what they all have in common is the cozy warmth of a wooded home. Over-sized windows are often used to counterbalance the heaviness of the wood by bringing in lots of light. Integrated outdoor living spaces are common, as well.

Contemporary-style cabins use clean lines and minimalist interiors. A single sloping shed roofline is typical. Modern Scandinavian cabins are similar but tend to use a simple gable roof, which blends traditional rustic with modernism. Open, airy floor plans are paired with white or light wood colors for walls and floors for refined simplicity.

Traditional-style tiny log cabins are readily available as kits and pre-fabs. Prefab or modular cabins are built in a factory and delivered in one piece or in multiple pieces to be assembled on-site. Of course, custom-built cabins are available, too. Choose from different kinds of logs: organic-feeling handcrafted logs, precision-cut milled logs with a uniform, smooth look, or log siding that can transform a stick-built house into a log cabin.

Ultimately, whether you prefer a sleek modern or classic country feel, there's a tiny cabin design for you.

COTTAGES

A cottage is a small single-story house, often in the countryside. This old-world modest dwelling style evokes enchanted homes found in fairy-tales. The origins trace back to the housing of peasant farmers, or "cotters," in medieval England, with quaint thatched-roof cottages. Layers of dry long-stemmed plants such as wheat and straw were carefully crafted to form a surprisingly durable, insulative roof. Poor farmers made their modest homes from readily available materials, yet a sense of artistry also came through. What began as a practical home style has become stylish and desirable in the present day.

Cottage-style houses are found worldwide, from quaint dwellings to darling vacation rentals. There are several distinct designs. What makes each recognizable as a cottage is their small footprint, coziness, simplicity, and timeless charm.

A coastal or beach-style cottage is typically found nestled on the oceanside or shore of some body of water. An open, broad porch or deck is a top feature for enjoying the sea or lake breezes. Seaside-inspired colors and nautical decor details are commonplace. A coastal cottage uses durable, water-resistant materials to withstand the demands of the climate. Long, narrow wooded clapboard and board-and-batten siding are often used, typically painted with light colors.

A Tudor cottage has a fairy-tale feel with its gingerbread house-like steep gable roofline, tall ornamental chimney, and decorative half-timbered facade—exposed wooden beams showing in the exterior plaster walls. Although their roots are based in 16th century England, Tudor cottages are more closely related to early 20th century Tudor and English-revival architecture. You can also find numerous brick, stone, or shake-sided cottages inspired by the Tudor-style shape but sans the half-timbered styling.

Cottages tend to be asymmetrical, inside and out. Interiors usually feature exposed wooden beams and wood floors. Open shelving is often used to maintain an airy feel. Classic cottage home designs embrace a rustic yet elegant French country aesthetic or a shabby-chic down-home country feel. Think soft pastel or earth-tone paint colors combined with rich wood accents and a few eclectic vintage or rustic accessories to complete the look. Fundamentally, cottage homes tend to be full of traditional character with a whimsical flair.

A-FRAMES

Imagine a timeless small house that can fit perfectly on the coast or in the mountains. You might picture an A-frame, a triangular house with a giant roof that replaces exterior walls. There's something about the symmetry of A-shaped design that is so intriguing: It inspires both a child-like wonder and projects a grown-up romantic appeal. Maybe it's because A-frames look similar to evergreen trees that they feel so right nestled in the forest. With an architectural style that favors expansive window views, an A-frame fosters a sense of connection with the outdoors. The abundant natural light also generates household energy savings.

The iconic A-frame look exudes simplicity. It's no wonder there has been such a strong resurgence of this style during the height of the tiny-house movement. Further, the simplicity of structural poles leaning against each other to form the A shape harkens back to early human dwellings. Construction is relatively straightforward, especially for the less experienced builder.

Durability in the face of harsh weather is another significant benefit of A-frames. For cold climates, snow is unable to build up on the steeply sloped roof. It's also beneficial in warmer climates: the heat rises into the peak, maintaining a cool main floor. Keep in mind, all that roof means replacing it can get pricey. Plan to invest in a durable roofing material, like metal. This will ensure a long-lasting roof without much need for repairs, but the up-front cost is on the high end—$5 to $12 per square foot.

With any kind of tiny-house design, you'll need to get creative to maximize every inch. A-frames require many clever storage solutions because all the wall space is angled, which dramatically affects furniture placement, built-in storage, and decor options. (And those 400 square feet or less tend to have even steeper sloped walls.) You may need to pass on hanging artwork. Instead, embrace accent walls to add a pop of color or rich texture through elements like bright paint, bold wallpaper, or reclaimed wood. Browse Instagram and Pinterest for successful A-frame tiny house decor inspiration.

Another way to get ideas is to take a research vacation! Book a stay in various-size A-frame rentals to get a sense of the space in-person—a surefire way to figure out if an A-frame can work for you.

YURTS

Have you ever experienced a round structure? There's something about the organic shape that many find grounding. Traditional yurts are circular, tent-like portable dwellings that originated in Central Asia thousands of years ago. They were composed of a collapsible lattice framework with flexible poles covered by felt or other fabric. Mongolian nomads moved their yurts four times a year on average. It took about three pack animals to transport one and about two hours to take down or put up. In some cases, relocation occurred via yak-pulled carts.

Despite their portability, these yurts were remarkably sturdy, with colorful wooden doors and wood stoves. Brightly colored rugs covered the interiors for style, comfort, and added warmth. Even in harsh climates, where Mongols moved with their livestock herds, they could feel cozy inside and protected from windy conditions. Due to their round walls, yurts resist wind from all directions.

As the Mongolian empire spread across eastern Europe in the 13th century, so did yurt design. Modern yurts have become popular across the world as semi-permanent glamping accommodations or more permanent dwellings. Basic yurt design hasn't changed much, though. What is different is modern amenities, like windows, along with layout customization through partition walls. A center ring with an opening acrylic dome skylight replaced the traditional wooden crown. Yurt covers now come in a variety of materials: waterproof canvas, high-tech fabrics, or wood panels. Significantly increased interior heights now allow for lofted bedrooms, further maximizing the available square footage.

Most modern yurts aren't meant for moves. They are now typically built onto a sturdy wooden platform with utilities installed underneath the floor system. Year-round living, even in cold climates, is possible with a heat source and optimized insulation. Reflective insulation is added to walls and the roof in fabric yurts, and wood-sided yurts use rigid board foam insulation. Platform insulation is also critical. Many modern yurts are designed explicitly with energy-efficiency in mind with features like a venting skylight dome.

Tiny home yurts come in 12- to 22-foot diameters with heights up to 12 feet. Surprisingly, the total cost of a tiny yurt cabin kit is about the same as the fabric alternative because of add-on costs for windows, doors, etc. You can get a yurt permitted in parts of California, Colorado, and Hawaii. Full-time yurt living is best done in areas with no building code restrictions.

GEODESIC DOMES

A geodesic dome, or geodome, is a sphere-like structure composed of a complex network of triangular pieces creating a self-balancing structural framework. A dome home is a dwelling with standard features and amenities like any house, except in the shape of a partial sphere. Architect Buckminster Fuller invented the geodome back in the 1940s, intending to revolutionize the housing industry. He received a patent in 1954 and spent his life perfecting the design. Unfortunately, his space-age-looking geodomes didn't take off for residential use due to various complications with building codes, among other issues. Other architects and engineers later helped overcome code obstacles. By the 1970s and '80s, dome homes gained popularity as quirky alternatives to cookie-cutter mainstream housing.

A geodesic home is lightweight, cost-effective, and superbly energy-efficient. Due to its aerodynamic shape, a geodome can better withstand extreme weather conditions, like hurricanes. (Monolithic dome homes, steel-reinforced concrete structures, are even more durable.) Weight from a fallen tree or heavy snow won't likely crush it due to load distribution across the dome. Structural efficiency is built into a geodome's sphere-like structure; they enclose more volume with less surface area. Consequently, geodomes use about 30 percent fewer building materials, doing more with less—a concept dear to the tiny-house movement. It also has less total outside surface area compared to a boxy house, which means lower loss of indoor temperatures.

In a round home, airflow provides natural circulation. Air travels efficiently around the space instead of bouncing off walls, keeping energy consumption at a minimum. You can enjoy tremendous heating and cooling cost savings.

Geodome construction can be relatively fast and is do-it-yourself friendly, thanks to the many prefab kits available. You can build a tiny dome home shell for $5,000 to $10,000.

A geodome's open round living environment feels uplifting. High ceilings with skylights contribute to this feeling. Interior design, though, can be a huge challenge because of the inherent lack of flat walls and right angles. You can add plenty of interior walls to create right angles via careful planning. All domes, however, will have some unused space. Consider using these weird little areas for plants, custom closets, or shelves. You can also think of the dome home layout as a pie. Each room or living space is like a slice. Look up floor plans from kit manufacturers to get a sense for how the slices can combine to create a livable layout.

COB HOUSES

Cob is a natural home building style that uses sustainable, abundant organic materials. Popularity of this housing option is growing due to ease of construction and low cost. A cob house is made of soil, sand, and straw combined to create clay-like lumps. This simple earthen material is incredibly durable. The earliest existing cob homes are over 500 years old! The walls are built up with lumps of damp cob mixture, then compressed, and finally sculpted into smooth, curved forms, which allows for creative flexibility. Like a living sculpture, cob homes look whimsical with curvy organic shapes. Artistic designs with intricate detailing is another characteristic. For instance, it's easy to mold cob into curved arches, sloped ceilings, and even built-in furniture, like shelves and benches. Let your imagination run wild to create your unique version of a romantic cob cottage!

The fibrous, muddy cob mixture is porous, which allows the structure to breathe via its tiny pores. This keeps the air fresh, clean, and free of toxins, making cob houses an ideal environment if you suffer from indoor allergies. Despite its porousness, cob is surprisingly resistant to elements like rain and cold. It's also basically fireproof and not attractive to termites, unlike wood structures.

Cob house walls are incredibly thick, with two to three feet of insulation that helps temperatures stay consistent and comfortable. They achieve this by absorbing sunlight, which slowly warms the house throughout the day, known as passive solar heating. Typically, a cob house uses approximately 20 percent less energy to heat compared with a typical home. Most important, it stays warm in the winter and cool in the summer. Thick earthen walls also beautifully absorb sound, creating a kind of acoustic insulation. This keeps the cob house very quiet inside and out, blocking exterior noises and preventing interior noises from flowing between different areas of the house.

Cob house construction style requires absolutely no building experience. It's straightforward and easy to learn how to build yourself with a bit of research; see the Resources at the back of the book. However, it can be quite time-consuming.

Build a debt-free tiny cob home yourself for as little as a few thousand dollars. You use primarily inexpensive and free local materials. But, if you hire out, the overall cost rises dramatically due to its labor-intensive nature.

Zoning and the Tiny House

Building a stationary tiny house requires land. As a result, you are subject to local regulations regarding what you can build on it, how you build it, and other utility and setback requirements. Whether you already own property or have a dream lot in mind, your first step is to do your research.

There are two big questions you need to answer when building a tiny house on a specific land lot. How is it zoned, and what building standards are required? Zoning laws govern how a particular property can be used and what can be built on it. Building codes are regulations on what standards a structure must be built to—enacted by the state, county, and city governments.

Begin by identifying the land lot's exact location: Is it in a municipality (city or town) or in the county? Next, contact the appropriate community development department to get the lowdown on the property. This is the hub for zoning, building codes, and development-permitting requirements. Check the department's website for quick-reference guides on various topics and associated staffer contacts. Ask a planner, first and foremost, if there is a minimum square footage requirement for dwellings on the property in question.

Additionally, you'll need to inquire about any deed restrictions or homeowner association (HOA) rules. These can also govern what you can build on a particular lot. Believe it or not, some locales won't allow building a home under 900 square feet.

After establishing if a tiny house can be built on your property, you need to determine what building standards have been adopted by your municipality. Numerous states, counties, and cities have adopted the International Residential Code (IRC) Appendix Q for tiny houses. The IRC is a comprehensive code regulating residential construction for the United States. Appendix Q addresses the specific needs of building a home under 400 square feet, like ceiling heights. It also allows for sleeping lofts and alternative loft access, like a ship's ladder. You can build a tiny house even if the Appendix Q isn't in effect locally, but it'll add layout challenges. Do you want to build a tiny cob home? IRC Appendix U exists for cob construction, but a jurisdiction must adopt it to become a part of its building regulations.

Next, you need to look into other development requirements. You'll need to obtain permits for utility connections like running electricity to your tiny home and connecting to the city water and sewage system. In most cases, the cost to hook up water and power is $10,000 to $30,000. More rural locations will require drilling a well and installing a septic system.

All of the steps outlined above apply to building a tiny house as an accessory dwelling unit (ADU) or as a primary residence on your own land. Reminder: An ADU is simply a small second dwelling on the same property as a regular single-family house (the primary residence). Single-family residential zoning opportunities for tiny homes are limited within most city limits, and are slowly but steadily expanding for ADUs. However, multi-family residential options like cottage clusters are becoming increasingly popular and available. This is a group of small dwellings clustered around a common green space, also called a pocket neighborhood. Keep in mind, you'll most likely need to work with a builder chosen by the cottage community developer. The home price will be much higher because it includes land, infrastructure, and permitting costs. The big advantage is not having to worry about figuring out zoning and building codes on your own.

Ground-bound ADUs are most practical if you already own a single-family home. An ADU will increase your property value and provides an exciting opportunity to pay off your mortgage. Consider renting out the main house while living tiny in your backyard!

Unrestricted land is your best option for providing you the freedom to build whatever style of tiny house you like. Look for counties with minimal zoning and no building codes. However, essential health and safety regulations will likely still be required. Always check with the county to find out what rules and inspections are needed. See the Resources in the back of the book to help you find unrestricted land (page 125).

CHAPTER FIVE

UNCONVENTIONAL TiNY HOUSES

Human history is full of remarkably inventive shelters made from a vast array of materials. Using readily available objects to craft a protective shelter seems incredibly practical. But the first time a new kind of dwelling came into being probably seemed odd to other community members. Imagine being the first to ask, "I wonder what would happen if I wrapped animal skins around this grouping of sticks?" But necessity always spurs invention.

Thousands of years of home building have led to a set of conventional standards and house forms. Just wanting to live in 400 square feet or less is seen as unconventional these days. Creative and sometimes rebellious, people have always pushed the boundaries of what's possible in our society—and "home-making" is no different!

In this chapter, you'll learn about the tiny-house options that use unconventional materials, plus the benefits and challenges of each option.

Tiny-House Conversions

Creating a home from an atypical object, like a grain silo, requires vision. It may have a roof and walls, but that's where the similarities to a house end. Imaginative thinkers and tinkerers have come up with creative ways to transform the unexpected into something new.

Converting something built for an entirely different purpose into a home is complicated. You must remove any original parts that will get in your way. You then have to figure out how to add the features you need to create a cozy, functional space. Ready for the challenge? Let's explore intriguing tiny-home conversion types.

BUSES

Bus conversions have a long history in the U.S., first gaining notoriety in the 1960s. Back then, "hippie buses" featured wacky exterior colors and basic camper amenities. A cult following of "bus nuts" tinkered and perfected the art of the conversion over the decades. Now "skoolies" are widely popular homes on wheels.

A skoolie is a decommissioned school or shuttle bus upcycled and renovated into a motorhome. People use them as budget-friendly campers and, increasingly, as full-time homes. Skoolies are often viewed as a hybrid between tiny houses on wheels and traditional RVs. Similar to tiny houses on wheels, they make for highly custom, individualized dwellings. But a bus home comes with a tow vehicle built-in, making it even better suited for nomadic living. Unlike RVs, school buses are exceptionally hefty, designed to hold thousands of more pounds to accommodate seats and people. With proper maintenance, a retired bus in good condition can remain road-worthy for a long time—over a million miles for diesel engines!

Skoolies can seem fairly unassuming from the outside, but stepping inside reveals a stunning cabin or sleek modern home look. From bare-bones to high-end luxurious, conversion costs range from about $10,000 to $85,000, inclusive of the bus cost. The extensive price range is due to factors like size, bus age and condition, materials used during the conversion, and whether you do the work yourself or contract out. Anyone with basic building skills can comfortably take on a bus conversion. You can find numerous YouTube step-by-step guides, plus endless how-to information sharing in forums.

School buses range from 20 to 42 feet long with an average width of 7½ feet. Once you remove the seats, a bus is like a blank canvas that can be built out however you see fit. Create separate rooms, if desired, with basic framing. Kick your creative problem-solving skills into gear with design obstacles like wheel wells. Use one as a footrest below a fold-up table or position a built-in sofa over this clunky space.

Lower ceilings can cause challenges, especially for tall people. The average height of a school bus is six feet in the center—remember, bus roofs are curved! Taller buses do exist, especially in the shuttle bus world. Create more height, airflow, and usable space by structurally altering your bus. Roof raises can give you several crucial inches or even a couple of additional feet. Hiring a professional conversion specialist is your best bet for a safe raise. But be prepared to drop several thousand dollars. Also, unlike van conversions, it is much easier to build a fully functional bathroom in a skoolie, especially in mid- to full-size buses. Many skoolie designs split the bathroom into two small rooms on either side of the bus—shower on one side and the toilet, plus a compact vanity, on the other side to maximize openness and layout flow.

VANS

Is wanderlust calling you toward a nomadic lifestyle? A van conversion might be the best tiny home for you. It's undoubtedly the most cost-effective traveling home. But it's typically more expensive than a skoolie conversion because a van in decent condition costs more than a retired bus. Low-end van conversion cost, including a used van, is around $12,000. But with a new van purchase, you could expect to spend as much as $150,000 on your tiny conversion home!

Choosing a van is a critical first step. There are numerous types and models of vehicles out there. Some come with extra headroom or floorspace—even a few extra inches can make a huge difference in a van conversion! Sprinter-style vans are a popular choice for full-time living. Their long, boxy shape makes them well-suited for spacious, storage-rich interiors. Ample interior standing height for taller people is another top feature. Cargo vans also offer more roomy interiors but at a much less expensive price point. However, finding a used one with lower mileage is tough. Although stealth camping is risky, many people use cargo vans for overnight camping on the down-low, sometimes illegally.

After selecting your ideal van, plan your design and begin building out the interior creature comforts like a couch and utilities. Build your bed on a raised platform to maximize storage space underneath. An expanding couch bed is another space-efficient option. Adding a bathroom is one of the biggest challenges of any van conversion. Many go without one or only create enough space for a compact toilet because of extreme space limitations. Prepare to plan your daily life around access to public bathrooms at stores, rest areas, and trailheads. An outdoor shower can be mounted on the back of your van. Otherwise, you can rely on showers at campgrounds or truck stops.

Full-time van life is often portrayed as a way to live in nature. But don't let Instagram fool you; much time is spent managing work just like anyone else. Remote workers can enjoy the benefits of location flexibility with van life, as long as they have WiFi—or use a mobile hotspot. A van home is also commonly used as a way to escape high rents, meaning frugal van living in more urban areas. A 24-hour gym with showers and free WiFi can be a godsend.

Urban van life requires you to be constantly on the move, especially at night. There are more free overnight parking options than you might imagine, though not glamorous: under-the-radar residential parking, 24-hour Walmarts, commuter lots, and RV-friendly businesses like Cabela's and Bass Pro Shops. Beware of the dreaded knock on your window by a cop or security guard if no overnight parking signs are posted. Just be polite. You might just get a recommendation of where you can go for the night. Fortunately, there are many great apps now available to help you find free or low-cost parking—like renting someone's driveway!

SHIPPING CONTAINERS

Did you love building with blocks as a kid? The endless combinations are very much like what you see in container home layouts. Converting shipping containers into homes is full of fantastic design possibilities, from industrial modern to country cottage style. It's simply astounding what can be dreamed up with this unassuming building material. What at first appears to be a shabby steel box can be transformed into a chic home with a keen architectural eye and building savvy. Stack them, arrange them in L-shapes, or join them side-by-side to create a wide array of layouts and sizes.

It's also remarkably sustainable because it uses fewer precious resources, like lumber, by reusing materials in surplus. As you might imagine, the cost varies significantly by size and the level of customization and finishes. Transforming a single container into a tiny house is the most affordable option: A DIY can be done for as little as $20,000!

Used containers have hauled freight of all kinds. You can look up a shipping container's serial number to find out what has been transported in it. Avoid buying one that was used for toxic cargo. You must also inspect its physical shape closely. You can either look into it yourself or enlist a professional to check things such as structural integrity, degradation of steel due to corrosion, dents underneath and overhead, and information about past usage.

On its own, a shipping container is structurally sound and extremely durable. It's manufactured to withstand harsh conditions. However, once you start cutting holes for windows and doors, you can compromise the structural integrity. This is why it's important to consult a structural engineer when converting a container. Steel is an excellent conductor of heat, and a bare-bones container may not be able to keep your house warm in the cold months and will bake in hot weather. So proper insulation is essential for comfort and energy efficiency.

Shipping container homes can be tiny or large, depending on the number of containers used. In a small container home conversion, you can more easily enjoy a full-sized kitchen, a large bathroom, and even a spacious living area for social gatherings compared to many tiny houses on wheels. Whether you're looking for a minimalist modern tiny home or artistic custom cabin, it can be done with shipping containers. But remember, you need land!

GRAIN BINS

Grain bin conversions feel as though Dorothy brought back a magical invention from the Land of Oz. A grain bin is a metal cylinder with a peaked metal roof used for storing dry grain and comes in various diameters and heights. Countless old bins are no longer in use, providing a prime reuse opportunity. Repurposing a used grain bin into a home is an environmentally friendly option, and when well-insulated, it's energy-efficient, too. Airflow in round spaces circulates more efficiently, requiring less heating and cooling. High-quality insulation is a must, just like container homes, to properly regulate temperatures in a corrugated steel structure.

Bin costs fluctuate based on demand, location, and steel rates. Smaller used bins can go for as little as a few hundred dollars or up to a few thousand for newer models in top condition. A high-quality grain bin has a durable finish to prevent rust and other deterioration. You can find one at local farms, auctions, or specific for-sale grain bin listing sites. Before you can begin a conversion project, a bin needs to be moved onto your land. Some tiny home-sized grain bins can be relocated with a flatbed trailer. Otherwise, you'll need to disassemble before it can be moved; how-to guides for this process are available.

Dreaming up a livable grain bin house floor plan is definitely a challenge. Fortunately, you can refer to layouts of other round homes to help you wrap your head around the possibilities. A benefit of grain bin homes is the vaulted ceiling, making the small space feel so much roomier. Take advantage of the height by adding a sleeping loft or even a standing-height bedroom, depending on the bin size. Choose a space-efficient ladder or spiral staircase. For the exterior, adding a front porch can create homey curb appeal. A second story deck is another possibility, and you might be able to utilize the exterior ladder or stairwell that often comes with a grain bin.

SHEDS

A shed can be used for so much more than extra storage space. Convert one into an office, bar, or a widely popular "she shed"—a fanciful backyard retreat. A shed tiny house is an incredibly affordable homeownership opportunity. Buy an appropriate-size shed kit or prebuilt storage shed for $1,000 to $15,000. Financing is readily available, too! A bare-bones conversion might cost as little as $5,000. More luxurious versions, with taller heights and more creature comforts, cost closer to $40,000 or more.

A shed tiny home is much more straightforward compared to the other conversion options. Wooden shed exteriors already look like a house and already come with doors and sometimes a couple of windows. You'll need to add flooring, insulation, and electricity to make it a functional home. Buy one with skids or add them to help with relocation.

Choosing the right option is crucial for durability and comfort. Manufacturers build sheds of varying quality. You want to seek out 2x4 construction with studs spaced 16 inches on center, like a house. A shed with studs farther apart is less sturdy. Lofted barn-style sheds are an excellent option. They typically come with a covered front porch and higher ceiling to accommodate a built-in loft. Shed manufacturers commonly offer upgrades like residential-quality doors, double-pane windows, and floor insulation. You can easily add these features to a new shed or shed kit order. But it's more challenging to add these after the fact in a prebuilt shed. For example, to add floor insulation, you'll need to take up the existing flooring.

A shed conversion is best as an under-the-radar backyard dwelling on a property you already own. Typically, sheds are allowed as an accessory structure in backyards but not meant for habitation. Most areas don't require you to get a building permit for a shed either. You'll want to check with your local zoning and building departments to find out what's allowed. Keep in mind, sheds do typically meet building codes because of how they're made. But using one as a legal dwelling will have to get permitted and meet local zoning rules for ADUs.

A PROFILE IN TINY-HOUSE LIVING

Meet the "Backroads or Bust" blended family who lives in a 40-foot school bus conversion. It's the full-time home to wife/husband duo Shyla and Jonathan, their youngest two kids (of four), plus two dogs. Together they bravely live life on their own terms outside of limiting social norms. "Everything in our life is about freedom," Shyla shares.

Their alternative living journey began in a ready-made camper, which never felt quite right. Shyla and Jonathan discovered skoolie conversions, leading them to purchase a 1998 Bluebird TC2000 activity bus. "It came with a basement and lower miles because it wasn't used as much as a regular school bus," Jonathan explains.

Shyla and Jonathan completed the initial build-out in just nine weeks. Over the next year, they perfected their space for their family's needs. The result is an amazingly functional, comfortable, and beautiful tiny home. Every detail was handcrafted and thoughtfully put together as a team. Each room feels like a distinct space. The "big sacrifice to get the floor plan we have," Shyla explains, was by downsizing from a king-size bed that they've always had to less than a full-size bed called a "three quarter." The smaller bed gave them room to add a walkway between their bed and large closet.

Further, they achieved privacy between the master bedroom and the kids' efficient bunkroom via a sliding door. Because their older two kids only live with them part-time, Shyla put their bunks on the bottom. She explains, "We made it so their two bunks swing up out of the way and leave room for the younger two to have play space."

They live nomadically and almost exclusively boondock (off-grid camping) on public lands, which allows free parking in scenic natural areas for up to 14 days at time in one spot. Sometimes this means being out in very remote locations with little to no phone service. The two youngest are "road-schooled"—homeschool-enhanced learning through first-hand experiences at museums and nature excursions. When not on the road, the "Backroads or Bust" family home-bases from their land near Kansas City, where the two oldest kids attend high school.

The Challenges and Creativity of Tiny-House Conversions

Each tiny-house conversion has its specific limitations. But working within constraints often leads to more creative solutions. How can a beat-up old grain bin or school bus that has transported thousands become a home? The metamorphosis from one use to another is mind-blowing. Imagine how gratifying it must feel to craft a beautiful, cozy tiny house from a space that most others would never envision possible.

There are four musts for any tiny-house conversion: creativity, resourcefulness, adaptability, and strong problem-solving skills.

Begin with a plan. Planning is essential for any house building, but especially crucial with a conversion project because it's complicated. Building something from scratch is more straightforward and easier to wrap your head around. First, you must research your medium and familiarize yourself with the materials it's made of. What are the parts and pieces? Are there common issues you should be aware of? Look up how-to guides from those who've done it before. Take note of the pros and cons of different options, like engine or container types. The fun part of this stage is dreaming up tiny-house layouts. Watch YouTube conversion tours and create a Pinterest dream board. You can scribble rough floor plans in your notebook, for starters. Then use 3-D modeling tools, like SketchUp, to create a more mathematically accurate version.

Your conversion project is divided into distinct phases:

→ Research and planning
→ Build prep: creating a blank slate by preparing the original structure to be transformed into a home
→ Framing and rough-in: insulation, flooring, electrical, plumbing
→ Finishing and decorating

When you're ready to get started on the physical work, it's time to get dirty! In the build prep phase, you need to deep clean and remove any unnecessary components. The level of work involved in this phase varies based on the conversion type. A bus, for instance, requires that all seats and the old rubber floors be removed. Be prepared to encounter unforeseen challenges. Anytime you're working with a used structure, problems will arise. Your van could need a new radiator, or you might discover a big rust patch on your container. Before actually building, you need to make any necessary repairs.

With conversions, it might seem like your future tiny house comes halfway built for you. Don't be fooled! There are a thousand little steps needed to complete a safe build. Proper quality insulation of your floors, walls, and ceiling is crucial for a comfortable living environment. As you progress with your conversion, you want to avoid doing anything that can't be undone. Container homes are a great example. If you cut a hole for a window incorrectly, it is exceptionally complicated to correct.

Other aspects of the build have greater flexibility, like wall partition placement and living area layout. Consider a skoolie floor plan. An L-shaped built-in sofa can be placed in the middle of the front of the bus. This creates a sense of separation from the kitchen behind it while keeping the living space feeling open and airy. Alternatively, you could place the sofa on either side of the bus to create a long line of vision. If you can't make up your mind, no problem. You can take apart and reconstruct built-ins as much as you need to.

But when the time comes for installing electrical and plumbing, your decisions need to be more exacting. Decide very clearly where things like light switches and the kitchen sink need to be placed. Tape out placement options before committing. Changing these later on can be a beast of a challenge and might require some deconstruction.

Overcoming odd space and shape limitations goes hand in hand with a conversion project. A tiny one-by-six-foot space in a van, for instance, shouldn't go wasted. What can you fit here? Maybe a tall narrow shoe rack, with doors or latches to keep your shoes from flying around when you move. Building a bathroom with a rounded grain bin wall or a curved school bus ceiling is tricky. In the case of the bus, consider where the showerhead should be placed to achieve comfortable standing space. Sometimes you can map out your floor plan in a way that makes sense on paper but isn't practical in reality.

This is why it's essential to go with the flow. Don't get overly attached to a layout concept. During the build, make comfort and functionality your primary goals. Try not to get discouraged when your plan goes awry. A misstep or unexpected spatial puzzle is simply an opportunity to get creative. The limitations of your tiny-house conversion project are part of what makes it so remarkable.

CHAPTER SIX

MAKiNG It HAPPEN

Fantasizing about downsized living in a beautifully crafted tiny house is easy to do. Bringing that dream to life, though, requires some legwork and decision-making. Perhaps the most pressing decision you will have to make is whether you will buy your tiny home or build it yourself.

You can save a significant amount of money by building it yourself, but you must determine if it's actually feasible. Do you have the necessary skills or time? On the other hand, buying ready-made tiny houses is not as straightforward as it seems. Does the seller offer financing? You also need to vet the builder or seller to ensure the quality of the tiny homes for sale.

In this chapter, you will learn what it takes to build, purchase, and finance a tiny house. Let's explore your options!

Buying Preowned

Buying a preowned tiny house is ideal if you want to live tiny right now. You can cut out months of working with a builder or the complexity of figuring out DIY construction. With convenience comes limiting factors such as customization. Buying a preowned means missing out on all the major design decisions made when it was first built. But you can renovate to your heart's content—for an extra cost, of course.

AVAILABILITY

Tiny homes are a very small percentage of the overall housing market. So, anticipate a minimal selection of foundation-based tiny homes for sale locally. Your options expand greatly for mobile tiny houses that can be relocated. Transportation costs probably won't be included in the listing. If you're not up for towing it away yourself, look for a licensed and bonded professional hauler.

See the Resources section at the back of the book for online tiny-house marketplaces (page 125).

BUILD QUALITY

Whether you are buying a tiny house or a regular one, you should always inspect it in person before making the purchase. Not only is it a good practice, but it also allows you to understand what you are signing up for and how much renovation might be required. For a nitty-gritty inspection of the house's components and systems, you will want to hire a professional home inspector. This is standard practice for foundation-based houses, however this process is more challenging for a tiny house on wheels as it falls under personal property. That means it's up to you to investigate the history and condition of a for-sale THOW.

First, find out who built it and on what kind of trailer. A licensed contractor or certified tiny-house builder can provide more reassurance on the quality of construction. The next best thing is a self-build certification that requires clear documentation of the various build phases. Next, ask the current owner if they've experienced any issues with the THOW such as moisture problems. Look closely for any signs of mold or water damage when you do your walk-through. If you know someone working in construction, bring them along to look for any structural issues. Finally, the seller needs to be able to supply the trailer registration and title—much like buying a used car.

Ultimately, for beginners, the most reliable preowned tiny house on wheels might be one sold through a specialized, certified builder acting as the middleman for a past client. With a certified builder, you have a better chance of receiving a clear understanding of construction quality. And if any repairs are needed, the builder can take care of those for you.

COST

If you want a tiny house on foundation, the cost will be subject to the market's whims. A home's location has an enormous influence on its selling price. Even if the original build cost was relatively inexpensive, appreciation drives up the property value over time. As an area grows more desirable, the more expensive the house—tiny or not.

In contrast, the value of a tiny house on wheels depreciates somewhat over time because it's considered personal property. You might be able to find one in good condition for several thousand less than its original cost. Professionally built tiny houses tend to hold their value much longer than self-built homes because of quality verified through a proven track record and often certification. DIY certifications are less common.

Prefab and Kits

Prefab tiny houses are pushing the boundaries of home construction when it comes to environmentally friendly techniques and considerable cost savings. Short for prefabricated, "prefab" refers to the factory-built construction process. A prefab home is delivered in pieces and assembled on-site. You can choose from three main prefab types: modular, panelized, or pre-cut kit homes.

A modular home is built in large sections, or modules, off-site. The modules are then delivered to a home site and assembled together on top of a foundation and connected to utilities to create a fully functional dwelling. Modular homes tend to have a modern, boxy look due to the rectangular shape of the modules.

Panelized homes, in contrast, can come in many architectural styles. As the name implies, a panelized house is constructed from a factory-built panel system for the floor, walls, and roof. More on-site finishing work is needed than with a modular home.

Last but not least, a kit home is the simplest and most DIY-friendly prefab type. A kit home comes with pre-cut and clearly labeled components, delivered flat-packed with an instruction guide for assembly. Keep in mind that a kit typically creates just the shell structure, requiring extensive interior finishing. DIY building doesn't get any more straightforward than with a quality kit!

SUSTAINABILITY

A prefab tiny home gets high marks for sustainability due to its minimal construction waste. Efficient manufacturing of sections in a controlled environment makes this possible. Compared to extremely wasteful site-built houses, the environmental impact of a prefab tiny house is minute.

Factory-built prefab homes can also be more energy-efficient due to tight structural seams. This means less air escapes to the outdoors, making it easier to maintain the indoor temperature. Moreover, many prefab manufacturers specialize in eco-friendly offerings like net-zero-ready solar power and energy recovery ventilation systems. You can also commonly choose from green interior packages featuring sustainable materials, like bamboo flooring.

CUSTOMIZATION

Modular construction, generally speaking, has become quite sophisticated, with high-tech design and high-quality materials. But if you're looking for a completely custom tiny home, then you might be disappointed. In most cases with prefab, you will need to choose from standardized layouts. Customization typically means choosing from available finish packages and appliance upgrades. However, prefab kits and panelized homes offer an interior blank slate, easily customizable beyond the predetermined window and door placement.

COST

Affordability is the primary selling point of prefab tiny homes, especially if you are not interested in building from scratch. You get high-quality construction at a reduced cost compared to site-built houses—an average savings of 10 to 20 percent. This is mostly thanks to the efficient factory building process that requires less labor. Pre-designed modular homes also cut out the need for any architect fee, which can typically be 5 to 15 percent of the overall construction cost.

Note that the low up-front cost of a prefab tiny home does not reflect the final price tag. Plan for the additional cost of land and accompanying necessities, such as the foundation and utility hookup fees. And don't forget shipping expenses! First, there's the cost of transportation to your property, and then potentially a crane fee for placement.

If you get a prefab kit, you'll need to plan for even more on-site expenses. Depending on the kit, you'll need to budget for everything from interior finishes to plumbing. The more work you do yourself, the less the overall cost.

SPEED AND EASE OF CONSTRUCTION

Prefab home construction generally can be completed in just a few weeks to a couple of months. Factory building is efficient and protected from the elements, so there are no delays due to bad weather. Foundation site work can also be completed simultaneously. Keep in mind, if you choose a modular or panelized home, you might need the help of a contractor to assemble it to ensure the finishing work is done properly and to code. Ultimately, the completion of a modular tiny home can be relatively simple and might only require utility hookups.

When it comes to prefab kit assembly, you and a few friends could complete it over a weekend. Think of it like building by numbers. All necessary components come color-coded and numbered. Simply follow the instructions to put it all together. After completing your kit, or structural shell, plan for at least a couple of months to complete the interior—adding electrical, plumbing, cabinetry, etc.

PERMITTING

Believe it or not, most prefab tiny homes can easily meet or exceed local building code requirements for the shell structure. You will need to deal with your building department to permit your foundation and various stages of interior construction, which applies to kits and panelized homes. Modular tiny houses, on the other hand, often receive state-level building permits. Keep in mind, all types of prefabs must still follow local land use and zoning regulations.

A PROFILE IN TINY-HOUSE LIVING

Meet Tori, a Millennial shellfish biologist who wanted to become a homeowner but struggled with affordability. Ultimately, she discovered tiny houses on wheels and decided to build one with cash as she went—a debt-free homeownership approach. Tori accomplished her big goal with a final price tag of approximately $30,000.

When she embarked on her tiny-house journey, Tori had zero prior building experience. Her first steps to prepare for her build included in-depth construction research and attending a how-to workshop. But it was perseverance that made her successful. No matter how long it took, she was determined to get it done right. "Some of the most challenging parts of the build were not getting discouraged. So trying something, failing, and being willing to try again—and maybe again and again, until you get that perfect cut to fit right," Tori explained. Ultimately, it took her one and a half years of active building to complete her tiny house over a three-year period.

Tori's tiny-house design style is farmhouse modern. She installed white shiplap walls, dark window trim, and striking exposed salvaged wood beams to achieve this look. Tori also used aged, corrugated metal for her sleeping loft ceiling, which makes quite a statement for the entire home while also creating a sense of separation between the living spaces.

Tori has an empowering message for newbie DIY builders, especially women: "It's really intimidating going to the hardware store and asking for what you want and having people question you. I suggest you try it, even if it's something small to build, or just go to a workshop, because it's empowering . . . . Now I see things, and you know, 'I think I can build that. I should try that.' It's a really nice feeling not needing to find people to do things for you."

Professionally Designed and Built

As the popularity of tiny homes continues to rise, so does the number of specialized tiny-house building companies. This is great news if the thought of building your own intimidates you or if you don't have time to research how to do it—not to mention the months to actually build one. Relying on the expertise of a professional is a true stress reliever. As a result, you can spend more of your energy focusing on the fun stuff, namely design and decor.

Tiny-house building companies have various offerings and services. The most well-rounded options offer complete turnkey service that covers everything from design, build, and permitting guidance, to transportation (if needed). Many tiny-house building companies have a team of architectural design and construction professionals to guide you through the entire process. Others offer only a limited selection of stock floor plans. The reason to choose a tiny-house specialist is to tap into their inherent understanding of a small space's challenges and how to maximize the limited square footage. Every builder's strengths are different, however. You'll want to shop around to find your overall best fit, from the right design capability to a price point that meets your budget.

MODEL VS. CUSTOM DESIGN

A big part of the tiny-living dream is being able to design a home tailored for you with cool custom features. When it comes to professionally designed and built tiny houses, the harsh reality is that customization costs money. Fully custom designs come at a premium price point.

Before you commit, browse available model home layouts. You are bound to fall in love with one of them. These are much more affordable than building a custom tiny home from the ground up. You can find ways to make it your own through decor and furnishings. No matter what, after you've lived in a tiny house for several months, you will find opportunities to perfect it to suit your needs better.

You may be in the enviable position of selling a large traditional house that generates hundreds of thousands of dollars. In a case like this, building a luxury tiny house on wheels or a dreamy remote tiny homestead is entirely within your means. Choose between a custom tiny-house builder or commission an architect to design your dream tiny home.

QUALITY

Perhaps the number one reason to go with a professional builder is to ensure that your tiny house is built right. The last thing you want is a major construction error to cause severe damage to your home, resulting in heartache and expensive repairs. Proper ventilation is a great example. An improperly vented tiny house can easily lead to excess humidity that leads to mildew and mold buildup.

In addition to proper construction techniques, a professional building company can achieve high-quality finishing work. From window trim to tile, these are the details that make a tiny house feel homey and high-end.

COMPROMISE

When hiring a professional tiny-house company, prepare to compromise on design, space, or cost. Your budget will dictate the level of customization possible and what finishes you can afford. For example, a luxury tiny house might be possible for you if it's 200 square feet smaller. You have to decide if it's worth spending more on size or the specific features you want. Also, do you have a brilliant design idea? A builder may burst your bubble by explaining it's impossible due to space limitations or another reason.

SHELLS

Looking to save more money but want to make sure your structure is strong? A tiny-house shell is the way to go. This semi-DIY option is ideal if you want a hands-on experience and interior customization. The shell comes with a complete exterior and a mostly unfinished interior.

A shell cost is comparable to a completed DIY build but significantly less than most professional models. The best part of a shell is that some of the most challenging aspects of the build, like framing and electrical, are already done for you. For tiny houses on wheels, many shells come with RV certifications and financing options.

DIY

Building your own tiny house is likely one of the most challenging and rewarding projects you'll ever take on. You can do it, no matter your experience level. However, it's not for the faint of heart and requires a tremendous amount of planning.

Is it worthwhile? For many, building their own home is incredibly fulfilling, both in the life-learning experience and the priceless satisfaction of living in a space built with your bare hands—an intensely unique sense of fulfillment. But deciding whether to pursue a DIY build, first and foremost, requires knowing what's involved in the process and assessing whether it's right for you. Once you have a better understanding of the pros and cons, you'll be empowered to move forward, or choose another path.

COST SAVINGS AND TIME COMMITMENT

Hands-down, the most affordable tiny house is one you build yourself. By not hiring out for labor, you can save 30 to 50 percent on the overall construction cost. Keep in mind, the final price varies considerably based on size and materials used. On the low end, a self-built tiny house can range between $20,000 and $40,000. Typically, a DIY build requires you to pay in cash versus obtaining financing—more on that later in this chapter.

While the savings can be huge, a DIY tiny house build will require months, or even years, of your life to complete—not to mention the stress involved in figuring out how to accomplish an unfamiliar and complex project. Starting and stopping when you get stuck on a difficult task, like roofing, can add even more time to an already slow build. Fortunately, there are more tiny house how-to building guides, workshops, and YouTube videos than ever before.

Even so, if you're new to building, the reality is that you will make mistakes that need to be fixed, which extends your overall timeline and can require additional material expenses. Do not be afraid to ask for or hire help. For example, ensuring your electrical is done to code is worth the cost of a licensed electrician.

Here are some factors that affect the construction schedule:

→ **Available up-front funds.** Can you cover the entire build cost, or will you pay for it over time?

→ **Time to build.** Can you dedicate every weekend and most weekday evenings to building?

→ **Your skill level.** Do you have any building experience, or do you need training?

→ **Support team.** Do you have skilled friends or family members who can help from time to time?

→ **Available time.** How long it takes to build a tiny house varies based on your situation, but generally speaking, plan on a year.

WHERE CAN YOU BUILD?

If you're planning on a DIY tiny house on wheels, access to a building site as well as tools are necessary. If you're lucky, you can rely on a family member with an available driveway or backyard. Just remember to make sure there's enough space to tow the completed THOW off the property! Discuss and determine ground rules, like not hammering after 9 p.m., to be respectful to the neighbors. You'll also want to be aware of any HOA regulations.

Otherwise, you will need to seek out potential build sites. Network through local tiny-house meetup groups for available yard space, or place a wanted ad on Craigslist and Facebook groups. You can also cold-call salvage yards and local farms to see if they have extra space they'd be willing to rent you.

Kill two birds with one stone by building at a Makerspace. These often offer both building sites and access to a wide array of tools for a monthly fee. Plan on at least a couple hundred dollars a month, if not more. Bonus: You can also enjoy a sense of community, with free-flowing advice and moral support from other makers.

BUYING PLANS

When you go the DIY route, beginning with a set of architectural plans (typically $100 to $600) can help you figure out how to accomplish challenging aspects of your build. For instance, they provide go-by dimensions for critical elements of the structure, like framing. From this starting point, you can more easily add or subtract space for any customizations. Another benefit of architectural plans is the standard inclusion of a materials list that can help you determine approximate build costs.

When shopping for tiny-house plans, look for those that have a proven track record. Check with the seller to confirm if they've been used previously for successful builds. Untested plans can be a risk. Sourcing your plans from a qualified professional will help ensure that quality standards have been met.

Purchasing professional architectural plans also helps tremendously with constructing a building code–compliant tiny home. Of note, a THOW can be built to meet RV standards, residential codes (from the trailer up), or both.

USING RECLAIMED MATERIALS

One of the best ways to save money, and reduce your tiny home's impact on the planet, is sourcing reclaimed construction materials. These previously used goods have been salvaged from a building to be reused in another structure. Find free and reduced-cost items in places like Facebook Marketplace, used building supply stores, and salvage yards. Keep in mind, finding the right reclaimed materials is time-consuming.

WORKING WITH AN ARCHITECT, CONTRACTOR, OR DESIGN/BUILD FIRM

Hiring a team to design and build your tiny house can be as simple as a Google search and phone call. But you may need to do more thorough homework to ensure you are hiring a trusted partner and the best fit for you. Top considerations include quality of work, customer service, and trustworthiness.

The world of tiny houses on wheels is far less regulated than traditional home building because code compliance is optional. Unfortunately, that can be a breeding ground for shady operators who post pictures of other people's work and claim it as their own. Do your due diligence when vetting a potential builder to avoid getting ripped off or receiving subpar work. Take these steps to help guide the hiring process:

- Check online reviews on Google and social media. But take them with a grain of salt; there are always two sides to a story.
- Check the Better Business Bureau for complaints.
- Ask the builder for references.
- Do your own research about basic tiny house–building concepts and certification programs to help you ask informed questions.
- Contact multiple building companies to compare quotes and customer service first impressions.
- Always get a legally binding contract, and never pay for all of it up front!

Hiring a licensed architect and contractor is less risky. With that said, thorough vetting is still a good idea. An architect can help you flesh out layout ideas and set realistic expectations for what's possible. Their expertise can be invaluable for how to solve spatial puzzles and for adding intriguing design features. Completed technical drawings will provide the basis for permits and guide the contractors on-site.

An architect can also guide the project to completion. Ask if they have any long-standing relationships with trusted contractor partners, which is quite common. An architect can provide project management, timing, and permit process guidance. However, find out what the architect is willing to do in advance and what they expect you and the contractor to handle. For example, an architect might choose and buy all the fixtures and finishes for your tiny house after consulting with you. On the other hand, you might figure out most of these details on your own. Either is fine, but make sure you are clear on expectations up front.

Securing Financing and Insurance for Your Tiny House

The process of financing and insuring tiny houses is getting easier all the time. With a decent credit score, you can secure a loan for all or part of your build. The downside is the higher interest rates and shorter terms. You can readily insure a tiny house, but the type of policy you need depends on how the house was built and how you use the home.

FINANCING FOR TINY HOUSES

How are you going to pay for your tiny house? Can you shell out the whole amount up front? Maybe you're lucky enough to be able to utilize savings or the profits from selling a larger home. If that doesn't describe you, you may need financing assistance.

The kind of loan you qualify for varies based on the type of tiny home. Short-term construction loans can be used for prefab and site-built tiny houses. You will need a good credit score, 20 percent down payment, and steady income. If you qualify for a government-backed loan, the required down payment could be as low as 3 percent. Keep in mind, your loan will need to be large enough to factor in all the costs of construction—house, land purchase, and infrastructure needs. Once the home is complete, you can convert your loan into a traditional mortgage. Some lenders offer a bundled version: a construction-to-permanent mortgage loan.

Do you already own a traditional house? Contact your mortgage banker about a home equity line of credit to finance a foundation-based accessory dwelling unit (ADU). It's a line of credit using your home as collateral and often has a low interest rate that may be tax-deductible. This financing option makes the most sense for those who want a tiny home as a vacation rental. This could also work well if you decide to live in the tiny house in the backyard and rent out the main house.

Only a few select lenders currently offer loans for tiny houses on wheels. They come in two primary categories: RV and unsecured personal loans. Both are very similar; neither option requires you to post any collateral to guarantee the debt. Instead, qualifying is based on your creditworthiness. A few lenders do accept fair credit scores, but most require good to excellent—the better your credit, the lower the interest rate. Note: Using an RV or THOW as a primary residence creates complications for RV lending. For some people, the solution is not disclosing their full-timing plans to the lender. If that idea feels uncomfortable, this option may not be right for you.

Personal loans come with great flexibility on how they can be used and few restrictions. You can easily find personal loans through a wide variety of peer-to-peer lending companies. Unlike a typical 30-year mortgage, personal loan payment terms are shorter, between five and 15 years. Borrow between $5,000 and $100,000, sometimes with no down payment required. Unsecured personal loans can be acquired by a DIY builder or through a tiny house–building company.

A few select banks also offer certified tiny house–specific financing via secure loans. Enjoy terms up to 23 years, which results in lower monthly payments. To be eligible, you must have a good credit score and pay a 20 percent down payment. Your tiny house acts as collateral to guarantee the loan. It's basically the same as an RV loan, except that the lender understands that the structure is intended for use as a full-time dwelling.

Nonprofit grant programs and rent-to-own programs exist for those unable to come up with a 20 percent down payment or are low-income. See the Resources section at the back of the book for a provider list (page 125).

Rent-to-own tiny houses do exist but are pretty rare. In a nutshell, a rent-to-own agreement allows you to rent a home for a set period before gaining ownership or simply provides the option to buy the house. While the contract specifics vary, part of your rental payments goes toward your down payment for the big purchase at a later date.

INSURING YOUR TINY HOUSE

Every home needs homeowner's insurance to protect it and your belongings from fire, accidents, and theft. If you need a mortgage for your tiny house on foundation, homeowner's insurance will be required.

Tiny house on wheels lenders, in contrast, don't typically require insurance. But if you want to protect your investment, don't skip it! Not that long ago, THOW dwellers were limited to RV insurance. RV insurance is best suited for nomadic homes on wheels. To qualify, you will need an RV certification mostly accessible through certified builders. A couple of self-certification programs now exist for DIY tiny houses.

Similar to auto policies, RV policies provide collision, content protection, and liability coverage. Technically, recreational vehicles are not intended for full-time living. Many insurance companies, consequently, stipulate this condition. Specialty coverage for "full-timing" is available by some insurers at a premium price point.

An increasing number of insurance companies now recognize the growing trend of tiny homes on wheels and are covering them under a "tiny homeowner's insurance." Unlike traditional home insurance, you will need one or more policies to cover the various aspects and risks of living in a home on wheels—the structure, your belongings, transportation, theft, and liability (if a visitor hurts themselves in your THOW). The costs associated with each add up, so unfortunately, tiny homeowner's insurance can cost as much as conventional home insurance.

The good news is that tiny homeowner's insurance is available for both professionally built and DIY homes—though, some carriers require THOW certification. Always make sure to read through all the guidelines and requirements to ensure you are in full compliance. Keep in mind, insurance companies may deny your claim if they find out later on that you failed to meet all their specified requirements to guarantee coverage. See the Resources section at the back of the book for a list of tiny house insurance brokers (page 131).

Tiny homeowner's insurance often comes with the condition that the house be on a semi-permanent foundation or at least tied down via a heavy-duty strap and anchor system. If you're planning to relocate, you will need specific trip coverage, called a trip endorsement. Otherwise, your structural policy will not cover damage caused by accidents during transit. Secure your trip endorsement through a tiny house insurance broker. You can also get it through an auto insurer, but they only offer basic liability coverage. If you hire a professional hauler, their rate typically includes general liability and cargo insurance, which will cover damage to your THOW. Be sure to review the coverage policy for any exclusions and limitations carefully. Secure a renter's insurance policy if you need additional coverage for your belongings.

An alternative insurance for mobile property is inland marine insurance. It's business insurance to cover equipment and goods transported by truck or train. While it can be applied to a THOW, it doesn't protect personal belongings or cover liability.

Before you consider pursuing tiny house on wheels ownership, it is best to consider how often you want to move to help you determine the kind of insurance most suitable for your lifestyle. After all, you want to protect your financial investment in the best possible way.

CHAPTER SEVEN

DOWNSIZING FOR A TINY HOUSE

Living with less in a tiny home does not mean sacrificing all creature comforts. Very few people find "Spartan minimalism" fulfilling, which involves owning the bare minimum, like only two sets of clothes and one set of dishes.

If there's one thing the tiny house movement embraces, it's living life on your own terms. Downsizing is no different. What feels right to you is most important, but you must push yourself to evaluate the clutter in your life. Downsizing is a necessary process of unburdening yourself from all the things holding you back by cluttering your space and mind.

If you are seriously considering living in a tiny home, this chapter will show you how to purge the baggage that can distract you from the benefits of a minimalist lifestyle.

The Liberation of Downsizing

The beauty of consciously simplifying is that it helps you get down to the essence of who you are. When going through a big transition, profound reflection is required to break through to the other side. Forcing yourself to sit alone and process your feelings about each of your belongings is essential. Often, we don't realize the emotions attached to our things. They might not have much to do with the actual object itself. In this way, downsizing can be a healing process. When you let go of physical clutter, you can also process emotional clutter that clouds your perspective. You might be surprised to discover that minimizing your possessions helps you uncover or clarify your priorities. How high does your stuff rank in your list of priorities? You'll likely reaffirm what you already know: Building strong relationships and creating memorable experiences are much more important than accumulating stuff.

Downsizing is all about identifying what's essential to your life. When it comes to belongings, ask yourself, "What do I need for day-to-day life?" Then, as Marie Kondo would say, "Does it spark joy?" Things that deeply resonate with you, like your favorite books, can be accommodated in a tiny house. You can design around what you most love and need. In our experience, simple living builds deep gratitude for what we have because it raises awareness of the essential role it plays in helping us survive and thrive.

Getting rid of excess stuff not only prepares you to live tiny but helps you embrace a more fulfilling way of life. Downsized living in a tiny home leaves room in your life to focus on your life goals, however big or simple they may be.

Where Do I Start?

Let's face it, beginning the downsizing process is daunting. Eventually, you will reach a tipping point when it becomes addictive, but initially it will feel like a hard slog.

The first step is to just get going! Procrastinating easily happens, especially when contemplating how to realistically fit your life into 400 square feet. Accept that you will end up saying goodbye to things you like. Sacrifice is part of the process. Paring down to the essentials is a necessary step of the tiny-house lifestyle.

You may be tempted to set overly ambitious goalposts for how quickly you'll be able to breeze through downsizing, but this will likely lead to disappointment. Starting slow is key, but stick with it.

Here are some techniques to guide you through the process one step at a time.

SORT ONE ROOM AT A TIME

Focusing on one room at a time allows you to ease into downsizing and avoid feeling overwhelmed. Give each room in your current home a first pass. Look for obvious things you can discard and throw them away.

Next, time for a second pass of each room to dig a little deeper. Now's the time to sift through and touch everything. Remember, it doesn't have to be done all at once. Try setting aside three times a week. One room may take just three sessions and another may take an entire month.

Hold each and every item: clothes, toiletries, books, etc. Pause for reflection, then label it as keep, discard, or maybe. Further sort the discard pile into donate, sell, or trash categories. You will further refine your keep and maybe piles later on.

Track your keep and maybe piles by clearly labeling them. You can also take photos to organize in folders on your phone. This is ideal for items too large to go in a pile, such as a couch. Remember, your keep pile is stuff you use, so make sure it's all readily accessible. Once a month, evaluate and note how often you used these items so that you can know their value to you.

The more you sort, the more you might realize that you can get rid of a lot with minimal heartache. It's incredible the clutter we collect over the years without even realizing it! Going through this process may also lead you to find precious items that you had misplaced or forgotten about. Consider this: If you haven't thought about an object for a long time, do you really need it?

BACKWARD HANGERS

Getting rid of clothing is a real sticking point for a lot of people. From fashion lovers to clothing hoarders, saying goodbye to even decades-old items can feel heartbreaking. It's important to note that you can accommodate a healthy wardrobe in a tiny house. However, you'll need to purge clothes that don't get worn often, or ever, to make room for your favorites and must-haves.

This is where the backward hangers hack comes in handy. Track what you wear by turning all your hangers around the wrong way. Over the next several months, as you wear something, turn the hanger around in the right direction. After a few months, you'll really start noticing what you're not wearing. Donate or sell these items! Keep in mind, this is most accurately accomplished if done seasonally.

SENTIMENTAL SORTING

One of the tenets of minimalism is to surround yourself with only those items that have a purpose or that give you joy. Thus, it can be challenging to decide what precious memorabilia items to take into your tiny home.

Is holding on to the physical item necessary for preserving those memories? Often, sentimental belongings stay hidden and even forgotten in a chest or cluttered closet. Actively reviewing these items brings back faded memories. As you sort your memorabilia, take time to reminisce. You will remember stories that you may not have thought about for a long time.

Try holding each item and asking yourself if it brings you joy or if it has a specific purpose that will be useful in your new home. If you can't say "yes" to either of those questions, you may want to leave it behind. But there's no need to rush or get rid of everything.

You can preserve the memory associated with a very sentimental item by writing about it in a journal with an attached photograph, or just taking a photo of it. This frees you to discard the item while retaining either the written-down memory or the visual that triggers the memory.

When sorting through your sentimental items, make sure that you're taking full advantage of the technology that's now available. Instead of a physical journal, consider a digital alternative such as a simple Word document or a journaling app. You may still have lots of home videos, photos, or documents as hard copies. Keep some treasured physical albums but digitize the rest through scanning or hire a digitizing company.

Another approach for sentimental items you wish to keep is to make them visible in your tiny living space, so you can truly cherish them daily. This can be a creative design challenge!

EMPTY A ROOM

Have you hit a downsizing roadblock? Intentionally clutter your space to snap you out of it. Empty the items from one room into the rest of your house, wherever you can fit them. You will create an annoying amount of clutter as a result. On the upside, this practice will likely help you gain clarity on what's essential to you and what won't work in your future tiny house—like a bulky dresser. What do you want to get rid of after a week or month of living like this? Move those items back into the empty room for your giveaway or sell piles.

STICKER TRACKING

Track what appliances and furniture you use most often with simple dot stickers. Do you really need a microwave, pressure cooker, stovetop, and oven? Simply place a sticker on an appliance every time you use it. Do this for a month or more. This exercise will help identify what is worth keeping. For example, you might realize you use your stovetop and pressure cooker much more than the microwave and oven. You might also require smaller versions of the appliances and furniture you wish to keep.

KEEP OR GO?

Once you reach the final rounds of sorting, you'll need to confront your keep and maybe piles. Deciding what to keep and let go of is incredibly personal. With that said, use this checklist to help further evaluate what's essential and realistic. Don't hold on to something that you might use one day. Wishful thinking is a clutter trap. Let go and feel free!

Kitchen

- How often do you cook, and what do you use most frequently?
- How many sets of dishes do you really need?
- What's your favorite cookware?
- Do you have any unused pots and pans? Or duplicate cookware?
- How much Tupperware do you actually use?
- What appliances and kitchen accessories do you use least frequently?
- Do you own any single-use appliances for nonessential cooking? (Think popcorn popper, waffle iron, ice cream maker.)
- How much kitchen storage will you have in your tiny house?

Clothes

- Does it fit you?
- How often do you wear it? And how many of one thing do you need?
- Are you only holding on to it because Grandma gave it to you?
- Is it stained or ripped?
- Do you love it?
- How big will your tiny-house closet be?

Toiletries, Beauty Products, Medicine

- What do you actually use?
- What are your favorite beauty products?
- What are you holding on to just because?
- Do you have any expired products?
- Where will you store these items in your tiny house?

Reading Material

- What are your favorite books that you can't part with?
- What books do you plan to read again?
- Can any physical books be replaced with e-books?
- Why are you holding on to old newspapers or magazines?
- How many bookshelves will your tiny house have?

Decor

- What are your favorite hanging artwork and decor items?
- Where will your decor items fit in your tiny house, and will they fit with the overall aesthetic?
- What decor items go unused and can be tossed out, such as candle holders in a drawer?

Linens, Bedding, Towels

- What haven't you used in the past six months?
- How many duplicates do you own, and how many do you realistically need?
- Do you own any ratty linens or towels that you wouldn't offer to a guest?
- How many throw pillows will look good in your tiny house?

Miscellaneous

- What craft supplies do you use regularly?
- Are you open to replacing CDs with a digital music service?
- Are you open to replacing DVDs with a streaming service?
- Do you have any old, unused computers, phones, or other audio/visual gear?
- Are all your audio/visual cables in use?
- Do you have any old manuals? Are online versions available?
- Why are you holding on to old school paperwork?
- What paperwork or photos do you need, and what can you digitize?
- How many pens and pencils do you actually need?
- What's in your junk drawer, and what have you recently used?

When It's Not Just about You

Downsizing isn't easy. But when you're single, at least you're in complete control of what should stay and what should go. If you have a significant other or kids, downsizing needs to be a thoughtful team effort. What seems nonessential to you may feel critical to another family member. Respectful communication is crucial throughout. It begins with discussing why you're doing it in the first place. What are you trying to achieve? You're more likely to be successful as a team or family if all parties involved can rally behind a shared goal.

DOWNSIZING WITH A PARTNER

Back in chapter 2, you learned that cooperation is the name of the game when it comes to living in a tiny house with others. That begins during the downsizing process. You must clearly communicate any frustrations that you're feeling about taking this on. Understanding where each person is coming from can help you work together to come up with solutions. Reading inspiring books dedicated to minimalism and downsizing can help assuage any fears about missing out on larger-scale living.

Is stuff more important to you than each other? Of course not. That's an easy baseline to agree on. Then, start slowly. Go through your initial round of sorting together. While you discuss each item, ask questions like, "Why do we need to keep this?" If you disagree, create a pro and con list to help come to an agreement. Prepare to compromise. Maybe you give in now on keeping something. In a future sorting round, ask your partner if they still feel the same way.

A fun technique is to pretend to live tiny in your current home. Think of it as a test run. Limit yourself to your bedroom, kitchen, and bathroom. Remove anything you both don't think you'll use daily. After a week, what do you each miss? And what is driving you crazy? Inconvenience and a little discomfort can test your communication skills and lead to shared clarity around what is truly essential.

Embracing downsizing as a team effort can make it easier. If you are undecided about whether to keep a personal item, ask your partner for their perspective. Be a support system and sounding board for each other. In this way, the downsizing process can strengthen your relationship.

DOWNSIZING WITH A FAMILY

Downsizing with a family can feel daunting. But turn it into a game for the best results. Asking your kids to give up toys might be asking for a tantrum, but if you can make it fun, you can avoid so much heartache. Begin by reassuring them that they can keep their most cherished belongings. Then, help frame their perspective around things they will say goodbye to by sharing intriguing possibilities. Maybe they can earn money by selling their things in a yard sale to save up for a fun experience. Or you might share how donated old books could bring joy to a child in need.

Downsizing as a family into a tiny home can feel more fulfilling for your kids if they get to be part of the design process. Listen to their input about what features they most want in their space. Do they want space for playing with building blocks or for their laptop? A fold-up table might feel really exciting to a kid. Watch YouTube videos together of tiny house families to get ideas. Ultimately, you want everyone to feel heard and like an essential part of the decision-making process.

GIVE, SELL, OR SAVE?

You made pile after pile of belongings you're willing to part ways with. Good job! Now what? It's time to meaningfully sort into sub-piles: give, sell, or save. There's no reason to throw away perfectly good things. Reuse and rehome as much as possible to avoid contributing to the landfill. Seeing your belongings find a new life can make the downsizing process more fulfilling.

Giving: If you're hesitant to get rid of old possessions because you don't feel they should be thrown out, find a good home for your stuff. Maybe a friend or family needs something you're getting rid of, like a sofa or Grandma's old china. And, of course, you can always donate to a local thrift store or homeless shelter. Be sure to check ahead to see what they will and won't accept. Also, receive a quality tax write-off by asking for a donation receipt.

Selling: A fulfilling way to process any lingering separation anxiety with your stuff is watching someone else excited to take on your excess and pay you for it. You can choose resale options, like Craigslist. Begin by further sorting belongings you're interested in selling. Identify your "top-shelf" stuff—higher value and desirable items in great condition. Any collectibles or specialized gear might be ideal for an eBay auction. Facebook Marketplace can keep sales local to avoid shipping costs. If you're not in a rush, physical and online consignment shops like Poshmark could be worthwhile. Setting up a flea market booth on weekends is another option. We made several thousand dollars to put toward our DIY tiny house build by doing this—but it took a lot of work! Yard sales are best for flash, everything-must-go sales. If you don't want the hassle, hire a professional to run an estate sale on your behalf. You typically pay them a commission. The convenience could be worth it.

Saving: Do you have items that you just can't bring yourself to part ways with? It may feel worth investing in some extra storage. There are many self-storage companies available that allow you to rent various-sized spaces, even closet-size lockers. If you invest in one of these, then you'll free up more storage space in your tiny home for everyday essentials. But all too often, items in a storage unit become forgotten. On top of that, you'll have another monthly expense to worry about. Paying $60 to $200 per month might make you eventually reconsider.

Strategies for Downsized Living

The tiny home lifestyle is all about simplifying to create a more fulfilling life. Not only can you enjoy a more freeing lifestyle, but you can lead a healthier one, too. Scientific studies have shown that clutter can cause chronic stress and weaken your immune system.

Quick and easy daily cleaning and organizing routines, as well as simply putting items back after use, go a long way in maintaining a small space that brings a sense of calm. When you're feeling a lack of motivation to clean, or an urge to over-consume, refer back to your "why," as discussed in chapter 1 (see page 7). It's easier to maintain a clutter-free home when reinforcing the reason you made this lifestyle choice.

KEEPING IT CLEAN

Keeping a tiny home tidy and clean is essential to your comfort in a small space. But is cleaning it as easy as they say? Yes and no. Overall, there is much less surface area to clean in 400 square feet or less. The flip side of that is you interact with most surfaces on a daily basis. As a result, a tiny house gets dirty quickly.

The easiest way to maintain your tiny home's cleanliness is to do a mini daily cleaning session. Dusting daily can prevent dust accumulation. With the use of an extendible duster or compact vacuum, you can effort-lessly manage to stave off all the dust on your place's surfaces. Since tiny houses do not come with a mudroom, they're more prone to dirt, grass, or leaves being tracked inside. So, everyday sweeping is a must. Another area to keep in check daily is the kitchen. A sink full of dishes makes the whole space feel messy. The best way to manage this is to immediately wash and put away these after use. Overall, a tiny home collects dirt quickly, but cleaning tasks can be done quickly, too. It will only take a few minutes each day to keep it feeling fresh and clean.

KEEPING IT ORGANIZED

Organization is everything in a tiny house if you want to maintain peace of mind. It only takes a few out-of-place items to make your tiny house feel cluttered or even claustrophobic. The best way to keep it organized is to create a place for everything and put everything in its place when you are done using it. After all, you don't have the luxury to throw your shoes wherever you want. Having the shoes on the floor might mean your table can't fold down, which means you can't access the bathroom.

All tiny homeowners have experienced this chain of events at least once in their time, and it's better not to make it an everyday occurrence. That's why everything you own needs to have its own designated space to maintain order and an open feeling in your tiny house. Maximizing your storage space is essential for achieving this. Every nook and cranny is an opportunity. Use open shelves and hidden drawers to put things away to appear less cluttered. Multifunctional furniture maximizes efficiency. A sofa with storage compartments can be a perfect solution for bulky linens or off-season clothing. Build drawers or a full closet into your compact staircase. Enjoy getting creative with storage in your tiny house—the possibilities are endless!

RESISTING THE URGE TO ACCUMULATE

Most people tend to fill up every inch of their available living space. A tiny home helps combat the number of things we own by drastically limiting square footage. However, the urge to accumulate runs deep. It's easy to collect stuff, even after your initial downsizing, which can lead to a messy, dysfunctional tiny house.

Healthy shopping and collecting habits maintain simplicity. Avoid big sales like Black Friday that can lead to mindless overconsumption. Embrace an intentional shopping practice. When you do go shopping for yourself, do it because you need something or want to replace something with a better-quality item. Think of it as treasure hunting for the "just-right" thing—like the perfect frying pan. With this approach, shopping can be a more meaningful experience. Your limited space is precious and should be reserved for the items you truly love or need. Naturally, this lends itself to a quality-over-quantity mentality.

Even with good habits, clutter happens over time. The trick for maintaining a clean and organized tiny home is to always be decluttering. Regularly take steps to manage messiness such as not leaving a stack of mail on the counter. Also, twice a year, do a basic downsizing sweep. Look for anything you don't use.

A tiny home has to be simple and free of clutter to be functional. That's what allows you to truly relax and enjoy your beautifully curated space.

A PROFILE IN TINY-HOUSE LIVING

Meet Traci and Matt, empty nesters who downsized into a tiny house on wheels on their own property. "We've been here for 14 years, so we raised our kids in the main house," Traci shares. "One of the reasons that we wanted to move into a tiny house is to simplify, obviously, but also give us a little bit of financial freedom. So we figured, if we built a tiny house and lived in it in the backyard, we could rent out the main house . . . and the house could therefore pay for itself—relieving us of a mortgage payment. And of course, the utilities in a tiny house are so much less."

Both carpenters by trade, Traci and Matt were well-equipped to build their own tiny house. Matt led the framing, and Traci did everything else. Ultimately, they created a wonderful custom 10-foot-wide tiny house. Their lifestyle preferences and the realities of aging informed their design.

Traci loves entertaining guests. To accommodate social gatherings, she built a large deck and added two doors to the front of the house. "When you just have one door that goes into a space, you can end up with a dead-end mess of people," she explains. Between the doors is a beautiful wooden bar table under a giant window that opens up to the inside, revealing a matching interior table.

Traci also created a downstairs master suite. She wanted to avoid climbing in and out of a loft for trips to the bathroom during the night. An inventive triple set of pocket doors open in various space-efficient configurations to access the bathroom while maintaining bedroom privacy and an open layout. A loft and full-size couch provide sleeping areas for when their kids visit. Luckily, if they need more space for visiting family, they can stay in the main house that Traci's sister currently rents!

Enjoying the Tiny House Life

Learning to live with less can be incredibly freeing. A tiny-house lifestyle can actually open you up to living a "richer" life, crafted around what matters most to you. True success doesn't come from what you own or how big your house is. Instead, it comes from personal empowerment to pursue what brings you joy and contentment. Enjoying more free time through minimal maintenance and more spending cash from the reduced cost of living are vital ingredients for creating a fulfilling life. A tiny home can be a multitool to help you achieve your goals. More than that, it can be your sanctuary—an antidote to the overly busy outside world.

Remember, simple living isn't about sacrificing everything you love to be the most minimalist you can be. Your tiny-house design can be tailored around your needs and what you genuinely love, even if that includes a shoe collection.

By choosing to live in a tiny home, you'll inevitably face naysayers. Prepare for a long list of questions and some criticisms about your decision. Just the thought of downsizing into 400 square feet is enough pressure. So learn to ignore critics or introduce them to shows like *Tiny House Nation*. The adorability of tiny-house design can soften negative views. And once they see your completed mini home, they'll likely change their tune. At the end of the day, you shouldn't entertain negative energy if you've already decided a tiny house is right for you. Knowing yourself and identifying your priorities are essential to crafting a minimalist lifestyle. This is about what's best for you—nobody else.

There is absolutely no better time than the present to prioritize your well-being and embrace more freedom. Start saving and continue researching. Consider how tiny you want to go, and whether you want to build a home yourself or buy one ready-made. If you can dream it, you can achieve it—we believe in you!

Are you ready to pursue tiny-house living? Dive into the in-depth Resources section for tools to help you on your path.

Resources

Downsizing: Books and Courses

Downsizing 31 e-Course (SmallerLivingHugeLife.com)

Downsizing e-Course (NicheDesignBuild.com/ecourses)

Downsizing for Life Afloat (SavingToSail.teachable.com)

Downsizing for Tiny Life by Chris DiCroce

Live a F.A.S.T. Life by Jenn Baxter

Minimalist Living for a Maximum Life by Emily Gerde

Simple Living Right Now by Brynn Burger

The Life-Changing Magic of Tidying Up by Marie Kondo

The Simplicity Master Class (CarmenShenk.teachable.com)

Tiny House, Rich Lifestyle Planning Workshop (TinyHouseExpedition
.com/e-learning)

*You Can Buy Happiness (and It's Cheap): How One Woman Radically
Simplified Her Life and How You Can Too* by Tammy Strobel

Design: Inspiration, Layouts, and Courses

101 Tiny House Designs by Michael Janzen

Building Your Moveable Tiny House with Mindfulness by
Patrick Sughrue

Cabin Porn: Inside by Zach Klein and Freda Moon

Compact Cabins by Gerald Rowan

Design Your Own Tiny House (ATinyHouseWorkshop.com/tiny
-house-design-exercise)

Idiot's Guide to Tiny House Designing, Building & Living by Andrew
and Gabriella Morrison

Jay Shafer's DIY Book of Backyard Sheds & Tiny Houses by Jay Shafer

Little House on a Small Planet by Shay Salomon

Micro Living: 40 Innovative Tiny Houses Equipped for Full-Time Living by Derek Diedricksen

My Cool Houseboat: An Inspirational Guide to Stylish Houseboats by Jane Field-Lewis

Online Tiny House Workshop by Andrew Morrison (TinyHouseBuild.com/workshops)

Pre-Fab Living by Avi Friedman

The Modern House Bus by Kimberley Mok

The Small House Book by Jay Shafer

Tiny Homes: Simple Shelter by Lloyd Kahn

Tiny Homes on the Move: Wheels and Water by Lloyd Kahn

Tiny House Design SketchUp Tutorial (TinynestProject.squarespace.com/resources)

Tiny House Design by Macy Miller (Udemy.com/course/tiny-house-design-part-4-custom-design)

Tiny Tiny Houses by Lester Walker

Vanlife Diaries by Kathleen Morton, Jonny Dustow, and Jared Melrose

Van Life: Your Home on the Road by Foster Huntington

Yestermorrow's Tiny House Design Classes (Yestermorrow.org)

Your Tiny Home Journey Starts Here Webinar (ExperienceTinyHomes.org)

Tiny House Plans: Architectural Plans and Custom Services

Den Outdoors (DenOutdoors.com)

Pinup Houses (PinupHouses.com)

Shelterwise (Shelterwise.com/store)

Sol Haus Design (SolHausDesign.com)

Terraform Tiny Homes (TerraformTH.com)

Tiny House Plans (TinyHousePlans.com)

DIY Building: Guides, How-Tos, and Workshops

Build Your Dream Van (DivineOnTheRoad.com/build-a-van)

Building Your Tiny House Dream by Chris Schapdick

Bus Buyers Checklist (NavigationNowhere.com)

DIY Skoolie Masterclass (DIYSkoolieGuide.com)

Go House Go! DIY Tiny House Building Guide by Dee Williams

LATCH Collective (LATCHCollective.com)

Shipping Container Homes: How to Build a Shipping Container Home by Louis Meier

Skoolie Academy (SkoolieAcademy.teachable.com)

Skoolie!: How to Convert a School Bus or Van into a Tiny Home or Recreational Vehicle by Will Sutherland

The Hand-Sculpted House: A Practical and Philosophical Guide to Building a Cob Cottage by Ianto Evans, Michael Smith, and Linda Smiley

The School Bus Conversion Network (Skoolie.net/forums)

The Tiny House BIG Book, a Beginner's Illustrated Guide to a Complete Tiny House Build by Abigail Ross

The Tiny Life (TheTinyLife.com)

The Wayward Home (TheWaywardHome.com/build-a-campervan)

Tiny Home Builders (TinyHomeBuilders.com)

Tiny House Build How-To Videos & Guides (TinyHouseBuild.com)

Tiny House Engage (TheTinyHouse.net/tiny-house-engage)

Tiny House Engineers Notebook: Volume 1, Off Grid Power by Chris Haynes

Van Build: A Complete DIY Guide to Designing, Converting and Self-Building Your Campervan by Ben and Georgia Raffi

Kits

Arched Cabins (ArchedCabins.com)

Avrame (AvrameUSA.com)

Conestoga Log Cabins (ConestogaLogCabins.com)

Den Outdoors (DenOutdoors.com)

Easy Domes (EasyDomes.com)

Econodome (Econodome.com)

Freedom Yurt Cabins (FreedomYurtCabins.com)

Jamaica Cottage Shop (JamaicaCottageShop.com)

Mighty Small Homes (MightySmallHomes.com)

Smiling Wood Yurts (SmilingWoodsYurts.com)

Sonodome (Sonodome.com)

Summerwood (Summerwood.com)

The Backcountry Hut Company (TheBackcountryHutCompany.com)

Volstrukt (Volstrukt.com)

THOW Trailers

Iron Eagle Trailers (IronEagleTinyHouseTrailers.com)

Tiny House Basics (TinyHouseBasics.com)

Tiny House Foundations (TinyHouseFoundations.com)

Trailer Made Trailers (TrailerMadeTrailers.com)

Appliances and Fixtures

A Tiny Good Thing (ATinyGoodThing.com)

Campervan HQ (Campervan-HQ.com)

Compact Appliance (CompactAppliance.com/tiny-house-appliances)

Composting Toilets USA (CompostingToiletsUSA.com)

Ikea (Ikea.com)

Shop Tiny Houses (ShopTinyHouses.com)

Skoolie Supply (SkoolieSupply.com)

TinyHouse.com (TinyHouse.com/shop)

Tiny Watts Solar (TinyWattsSolar.com)

Tiny Houses for Sale and Rent

Bus Life Adventure (BusLifeAdventure.com/classifieds)

Facebook Groups: Tiny Houses for Sale and Tiny House Classifieds

Tiny Homes Classified (TinyHomesClassified.com)

TinyHouse.com (TinyHouse.com/tiny-homes)

Tiny House Listings (TinyHouseListings.com)

Tiny House Listings Canada (TinyHouseListingsCanada.com)

Tiny House Marketplace (TinyHomeBuilders.com
/tiny-house-marketplace)

Tiny House Talk (TinyHouseTalk.com)

Vacation Rentals

Airbnb (Airbnb.com)

Blue Moon Rising (BlueMoonRising.org)

Caravan Tiny House Hotel (TinyHouseHotel.com)

El Pais Motel (ElPaisMotel.com)

Fireside Resort (FiresideJacksonHole.com)

Getaway (Getaway.house)

Glamping Hub (GlampingHub.com)

Hipcamp (Hipcamp.com)

Hummingbird Tiny Home Inn (TheTinyHomeInn.com)

Leavenworth Tiny House Village (LeavenworthTinyHouse.com)

Live A Little Chatt (LiveALittleChatt.com)

Mt. Hood Tiny House Village (MtHoodTinyHouse.com)

River & Twine (RiverAndTwine.com)

TinyCamp (TinyCamp.com)

Tiny Digs Hotel (TinyDigsHotel.com)

Tiny Home Vacations (TinyHomeVacations.com)

Tiny House Leadville (TinyHouseLeadville.com)

Tiny House Siesta (TinyHouseSiesta.com)

Tiny House Tryouts (TinyHouseTryouts.com)

Tuxbury Tiny House Village (TuxburyTinyHouse.com)

Villa Stay (VillaStay.com)

WeeCasa Tiny House Resort (WeeCasa.com)

Nonprofits with Affordable Housing and Grant Programs

Build Us Hope (BuildUsHope.org)

Cass Community Social Services (CassCommunity.org/tinyhomes)

Community First Village (MLF.org/community-first)

Habitat for Humanity (select local affiliates offer tiny home programs)

Homes on Wheels Alliance (HomesOnWheelsAlliance.org)

Low Income Housing Institute (LIHI.org)

Operation Tiny Home (OperationTinyHome.org)

Rebuilding Green (MovableTinyHomes.com)

SquareOne Villages (SquareOneVillages.org)

Tiny House Community Development Inc. (TinyHousesGreensboro.com)

Tiny Pine Foundation (TinyPineFoundation.com)

Tiny House Insurance

Foremost Insurance Group (Foremost.com/usaa/products/home-insurance/tiny-homes.asp)

Strategic Insurance Agency (MyStrategicInsurance.com/tiny-homes)

Financing

9 Financial Keys to Unlocking Your Tiny Dream (ContentedNomads.teachable.com)

eLoan (eLoan.com/personal-loans/tiny-house-financing)

Feeasy (ItsFeeasy.com)

Hearth (GetHearth.com)

Liberty Bank (LibertyBankOfUtah.com/tiny-homes)

LightStream (LightStream.com/tiny-houses)

Members Cooperative Credit Union (MembersCCU.org
/mortgage-loans/tiny-home-financing)

Tiny House Communities and Parking

Facebook Group: Tiny House Hosting

Search Tiny House Villages (SearchTinyHouseVillages.com)

Tiny Home Industry Association (TinyHomeIndustryAssociation.org)

Tiny House Expedition (TinyHouseExpedition.com
/tiny-home-communities)

RV Membership Programs

Boondockers Welcome (BoondockersWelcome.com)

Escapees RV Club (Escapees.com)

Explorer RV Club (ExplorerRVClub.com)

Family Motorcoach Association (FMCA.com)

Good Sam (GoodSam.com)

Harvest Hosts (HarvestHosts.com)

Passport America (PassportAmerica.com)

Thousand Trails Camping Pass (ThousandTrails.com
/membership-info)

Boondocking/Off-Grid Camping

Campendium (Campendium.com)

Free Camp Sites (FreeCampSites.net)

iOverlander (iOverlander.com)

Overnight RV Parking (OvernightRVParking.com)

RV Parky (RVParky.com)

Apps

FreeRoam (FreeRoam.app)

The Dyrt (TheDyrt.com)

The Vanlife (TheVanlifeApp.com)

Tiny hOMe (WanderingFootprint.ca/app-1)

Finding Land

Land and Farm (LandAndFarm.com)

LandFlip (LandFlip.com)

Land Is Home (LandIsHome.com)

Lands of America (LandsOfAmerica.com)

LandWatch (LandWatch.com)

Rural Vacant Land (RuralVacantLand.com)

Tierra Land Company (TierraLandCo.com)

Zillow (Zillow.com)

Tiny House Advocacy

Accessory Dwellings (AccessoryDwellings.org)

American Tiny House Association (AmericanTinyHouseAssociation.org)

Australian Tiny House Association (TinyHouse.org.au)

Backdoor Revolution by Kol Peterson

MicroLife Institute (MicroLifeInstitute.org)

New Zealand Tiny House Association (NZTHA.org)

Tent City Urbanism: From Self-Organized Camps to Tiny House Villages by Andrew Heben

Tiny Home Alliance Canada (TinyHomeAlliance.ca)

Tiny Home Industry Association (TinyHomeIndustryAssociation.org)

Tiny House Village Toolbox (SquareOneVillages.org/toolbox)

Tiny Town Association (TinyTownAssociation.com)

Towing Guides

Tiny Home Builders (TinyHomeBuilders.com/help/tiny-house -towing-guide)

Tiny House Build (TinyHouseBuild.com/how-to-tow-a-tiny-house)

Tiny House Expedition (TinyHouseExpedition.com/tiny-house-travel)

Trailer Life (TrailerLife.com/trailer-towing-guides)

Professional Hauling Services

Coast to Coast Transportation (TransportCoastToCoast.com/services /tiny-house-transport)

Heavy Haulers (HeavyHaulers.com/transporting-tiny-houses.php)

One Call Logistics (One-CallLogistics.com/tiny-house)

Tiny Home Movers USA (TinyHomeMovers.com)

Tiny Home Transport (TinyHomeTransport.com)

Tiny House Deliver Company (Facebook.com/tinyhousemovers.net)

Shows: TV, Streaming, and YouTube Channels

HGTV's *Tiny House, Big Living*

HGTV's *Tiny House Hunters*

The Minimalists: Less Is Now on Netflix

Tiny House Nation on Netflix

Drivin' and Vibin' (YouTube.com/c/DrivinandVibin)

Eamon and Bec (YouTube.com/channel
/UC4laAHbk8VSgmvB47tsd2XQ)

EnjoyTheJourney.Life (YouTube.com/channel
/UCuhIeTBsCysER-73DnGEegQ)

Exploring Alternatives (YouTube.com/user/explorealternatives)

Florb (YouTube.com/user/Dylanmagaster)

Fy Nyth (YouTube.com/channel/UCaLQEHLG8SPlICSdxyCGCXA)

Jennelle Eliana (YouTube.com/channel/UCaXEr4t_QBZBk3qlIlc2HRg)

Kirsten Dirksen (YouTube.com/user/kirstendirksen)

Levi Kelly (YouTube.com/channel/UC3hEhxxlq9OWXWp4t4uYXKw)

Living Big in a Tiny House (YouTube.com/user/livingbigtinyhouse)

Living Tiny with the Bushes (YouTube.com/channel
/UCXP69pn8qngsiF-g8MznOvw)

Matt & Paiton (YouTube.com/channel
/UCNMQWKKHDwhNGei5pYlGJGw)

Mortons on the Move (YouTube.com/c/MortonsontheMove)

Mr and Mrs Adventure (YouTube.com/channel
/UC9fSBF6leAEI2JOcFrM2Mng)

Navigation Nowhere (YouTube.com/channel
/UCJ5ZDQnM9AztB4HpIM-2mWA)

Number Juan Bus (YouTube.com/channel
/UC2-QYnV5dTCOdntxL6OlTgA)

Off Grid with Doug & Stacy (YouTube.com/c
/OFFGRIDwithDOUGSTACY)

Off the Grid with a Kid (YouTube.com/channel
/UCmGJABCNtIDVslGxrwftugQ)

Our Way to Roam (YouTube.com/channel
/UCxKmUwf9jh9QE6UgmPR_c6g)

Ramblin Farmers (YouTube.com/channel
/UCqVe-IYsLT9NS9F_tbLv2aw)

RelaxShacks (YouTube.com/user/relaxshacksDOTcom)

SeaTreeWonder (YouTube.com/channel
/UCQB5Il9MS4RWN8xejVlWQ-A)

The Capable Carpenter (YouTube.com/channel
/UC3eyhVHLqmNYsdUx5wlvGYg)

The Mom Trotter (YouTube.com/c/TheMomTrotter)

The Tiny House Project (YouTube.com/channel
/UC8mpOkFOaUllqAOmfBYLl6A)

This Tiny Journey (YouTube.com/channel
/UC37w_lhcCqLdtQ4nRZH-HHw)

Tiny Dreamer (YouTube.com/channel
/UCuOClSrVmT8nQhOnDOtxiBA)

Tiny Home Tours (YouTube.com/user/tylerdurdeno9)

Tiny Home Wild Adventures (YouTube.com/channel
/UCHOxkBZ6jpoCYsrgEsGEZIw)

Tiny House Expedition (YouTube.com/TinyHouseExpedition1)

Tiny House Giant Journey (YouTube.com/user/tinyhousegj)

Tiny Nest Project (YouTube.com/c/tinynestproject)

Tiny Towns (SHGLiving.com/series/tiny-house-expedition)

Where Is Brittany? (YouTube.com/c/WhereIsBrittany)

Zeppelin Travels (YouTube.com/channel/UCtA9_KrZQLVzUN
_OFovA8iA)

Documentaries

Living Tiny Legally docuseries (TinyHouseExpedition.com/living
-tiny-legally)

Simplife (simp.life)

Small Is Beautiful (SmallBeautifulMovie.com)

The Meaning of Vanlife (VanLife.com.au/the-meaning-of-vanlife)

The REUSE! Box Truck Tiny House (StayVocal.com)

Tiny: A Story About Living Small (Tiny-TheMovie.com)

We the Tiny House People (FairCompanies.com/articles/how-i-made
-we-the-tiny-house-people)

Magazines

Bus Conversion Magazine (BusConversionMagazine.com)

Simplify Magazine (BecomingMinimalist.com/simplify-magazine)

Tiny House magazine (TinyHouseMagazine.co)

Podcasts

Building Sustainability Podcast (BuildingSustainabilityPodcast.com)

Hope, Innovation & Impact Podcast (OperationTinyHome.org/hope
-innovation-impact-podcast)

It's Not a Tiny House Podcast (NotATinyHousePodcast.com)

Let's Talk Tiny Houses (LetsTalkTinyHouses.podbean.com)

My Solo Road (DivineOnTheRoad.com/solo-female-van-life-podcast)

Nomads at the Intersections (DiversifyVanLife.com/nomads-at-the
-intersections)

The RV Miles Podcast (RVMiles.com/podcast)

Tiny House Lifestyle Podcast (TheTinyHouse.net/thlp)

Events

Colorado Tiny House Festival (ColoradoTinyHouseFestival.com)

Good Vibe Collective (TheGoodVibeCollective.com)

Great American Tiny House Shows (GreatAmericanTinyHouse.show)

Open Roads Van Life Festival (OpenRoadsFest.com)

Rubber Tramp Rendezvous (HomesOnWheelsAlliance.org/2020rtrs)

Skooliepalooza (Skooliepalooza.com)

Skoolie Swarm

The Bus Fair (TheBusFair.com)

The People's Tiny House Festival (PeoplesTinyHouseFestival.com)

TinyFest Events (TinyFest.events)

Tiny House Community Calendar (TinyHouseExpedition.com/events)

United Tiny House Association (UnitedTinyHouse.com)

Social Groups

Choose Tiny (ChooseTiny.com)

Container Homes Facebook Group

Local Meetup Groups (Meetup.com)

Local Tiny House Facebook Groups

Shed to Home, Tiny Homes & Container Homes Facebook Group

Shipping Container Homes Facebook Group

Skoolie Planet Facebook Group

Skoolie-Nation Facebook Group

Tiny House Central Facebook Group

Tiny House Concepts Facebook Group

Tiny House People Facebook Group

TinyHouseResourceGroup Facebook Group

Tiny Houses and Off-Grid Living Facebook Group

Van Life Conversion Facebook Group

Other Books

The Big Adventures of Tiny House by Susan Schaefer Bernardo and Courtenay Fletcher

The Big Tiny: A Built-It-Myself Memoir by Dee Williams

Featured Profiles in Tiny-House Living

Marek and Kothney-Issa, Living Tiny with the Bushes (Instagram .com/the_bush_family_)

Richard, Terraform Tiny Homes (TerraformTH.com)

Shannen (Instagram.com/shannens_tiny)

Shyla and Jonathan, Backroads or Bust (Instagram.com /backroadsorbust)

Sol, Port Townsend EcoVillage (PTEcoVillage.org)

Tori (Instagram.com/tangled_tiny)

Traci and Matt, Big Bliss Tiny Homes (BigBlissTinyHomes.com)

Watch Tiny House Tours of All Profiled: YouTube.com /TinyHouseExpedition1

Index

A

Accessory dwelling units (ADUs), 43–44, 73
A-frames, 66–67
Appliances, downsizing, 113
Architects, 103

B

Beach-style cottages, 65
Bluewater houseboats, 42
Braking systems, 47, 52
Building codes, 72, 95, 102
Bumper pull trailers, 49
Bus conversions, 76–78, 86–87

C

Cabins, 63–64
Caravans, 40–41
Cass Community Social Services, 10
Children, 29, 117
Cleanliness, 119
Clothing, downsizing, 112
Clutter, 31, 120–121
Coastal cottages, 65
Cob houses, 70–71
Communication, 26–27, 116–117
Communities
    backyard, 10
    benefits to, 9–10
    RV and mobile home, 11
Concrete slabs, 58
Contractors, 103
Conversion project
        considerations, 85–87
Costs
    architectural plans, 101–102

buses, 77
DIY builds, 100
financing, 104–105
general, 3
grain bins, 82
insurance, 106–107
prefabricated, 94
preowned, 91
sheds, 82
shipping containers, 81
vans, 78
Cottages, 64–65
Crawlspace foundations, 58–59
Cruising houseboats, 42
Customization, 93, 98

D

DIY builds, 99–102
Downsizing
    with a family, 117
    getting started, 110–113
    give, sell, or save, 118
    liberation of, 30, 110
    with a partner, 116–117
    room by room, 111–112, 114–115
Driver's licenses, 47
Driving tips, 54

E

"Ecological Footprints of Tiny
        Home Downsizers, The," 7
Environmental benefits, 7, 93

F

Fifth-wheel trailers, 50

Financing, 104–105
Floating homes, 42
Foundations, 58–59
Fuller, Buckminster, 69
Furniture, downsizing, 113

G

Geodesic domes, 69–70
Going Places, 10
Gooseneck trailers, 50
Grain bins, 81–82
Grants, 105

H

Highway laws, 46–47
Hitch systems, 51
HOA regulations, 72, 101
Homestead Act (1862), 63
Houseboats, 41–43

I

Inspections, 90–91
Insurance, 106–107
International Residential
    Code (IRH), 72–73

K

Kit homes, 93
Kondo, Marie, 110

L

Legal considerations
    accessory dwelling units (ADUs), 43–44, 73
    building codes, 72, 95, 102
    federal laws, 46–47
    HOA regulations, 72, 101
    International Residential
        Code (IRH), 72–73
    state laws, 46–47
    zoning laws, 11, 43–44, 72–73
Liveaboard boats, 41. *See also* Houseboats
Living expenses, 8–9, 33
Loans, 104–105
Log cabins, 63–64

M

Maintenance costs, 8–9
Memorabilia, 112–113
Mobile home parks, 11
Modular homes, 92
Motorhomes, 37

N

Non-cruising houseboats, 42

O

Organization, 31, 120

P

Panelized homes, 92
Pier foundations, 59
Prefabricated tiny houses, 92–95
Preowned tiny houses, 90–91
Privacy, 27–28
Professional design and builds, 97–99, 103
Profiles
    "Backroads or Bust" family, 84
    Marek and Kothney-Issa, 45
    Richard Ward, 6
    Shannen, 32

Sol, 62
Tori, 96
Traci and Matt, 122

R

Regulations. *See* Legal considerations
Relationships, 26–27, 116–117
Rent-to-own, 105
RV parks, 11
RVs, 36–38

S

Safety features, 47
Sentimental items, 112–113
Shafer, Jay, 4
Sheds, 82–83
Shells, 99
Shipping containers, 80–81, 86
Simplicity, 8, 120–121
Skids, 60–61
Skoolies, 77–78, 86–87
Small House Society, 4
Storage units, 118
Sustainability, 7, 93, 102

T

Tiny (documentary), 5
tiny-house-living questionnaire, 14–26
Tiny House Nation (TV show), 123
Tiny houses
    benefits of, 7–10
    communities, 10–11
Tiny houses (*continued*)
    conversion projects, 85–87
    costs, 3, 91
    defined, 2

history of, 3–5
    as a lifestyle, 119–121, 123
Tiny houses on foundations (THOF), 58–59
Tiny houses on skids (THOS), 60–61
Tiny houses on wheels (THOW)
    communities, 11
    costs, 3, 91
    defined, 2, 38–39
    insurance, 106–107
    mobility benefits, 9
    parking, 43–44
    size restrictions, 46–47, 60
Tongue weight, 53
Towing capacities, 52–53
Tow safety checklist, 54
Trailers, 47–50
Travel checklists, 54–55
Travel trailers, 37, 41
Tudor cottage, 65
Tumbleweed Tiny House Company, 4

V

Van conversions, 78–80, 86
Vardos, 40–41
Veterans Community Project, 10

W

Weight capacities, 48

Y

Yurts, 67–68

Z

Zoning laws, 11, 43–44, 72–73

Acknowledgments

Thanks to Andrew and Sherry for saying "yes in my backyard" and kindly hosting our tiny home during the writing of this book.

About the Authors

 **Alexis Stephens** and **Christian Parsons** are tiny-house movement ambassadors and cofounders of Tiny House Expedition, a traveling documentary and community education project. They are passionate about sharing resources, events, and inspiring tiny-home stories with the world. Their work includes the documentary series *Living Tiny Legally*, an insightful resource for advocacy groups and policymakers.

In 2014, Alexis and Christian built their own tiny house on wheels with the help of friends and family. They hit the road in 2015 on a documentarian research road trip turned nomadic lifestyle, spanning 4½ years and 55,000 miles. Now, their filmmaking and event travels continue, part-time, in a shuttle bus conversion. Alexis and Christian also continue to live in their 130-square-foot tiny home and hope to create a mini-homestead in the future to host other tiny-house dwellers.

Tiny House Expedition has been featured by *The Washington Post*, *Business Insider*, *Parade* magazine, Curbed, *The Independent*, BBC Travel, HGTV's *Tiny House, Big Living*, HuffPost, Yahoo, Trulia, Treehugger, CTV News, France2, and NPR. Alexis and Christian share their insights at tiny-living festivals, schools, museums, realtor associations, and with local and federal government departments. They serve on the American Tiny House Association's board of advisors, and Alexis also serves on the Tiny Home Industry Association board of directors.

Visit their website at TinyHouseExpedition.com, stream their content on YouTube or SHG Living Network, and follow their adventures on Instagram, Facebook, and Twitter.